Dad's Guidebook: Finance

By Alex Molldrem

For my wonderful wife and loving family.

Preface:

It all started the day I looked at my bank statement. There, in the tiny print, I saw that I was earning 0.01%. Pennies. Finances was a scary thing to me, but there was no way I was ever going to be able to retire at that rate. So I decided to do something about it.

After years of reading finance books, making plenty of mistakes and wasting time along the way, I came to the resolution to write down the things I have learned. My goal was to provide a guidebook for my kids. I thought if they could learn some of these ideas 20 years before I ever did, it could slingshot their financial success. Thus the title *Dad's Guidebook*.

I finally put it all together, in what I hope is a clear manner, to share with you. It also gave me a way to use some great Dr. Seuss quotes. I hope you enjoy reading this, find it useful, and learn some valuable insights that have helped me along the way.

Who knows, maybe there will be a *Dad's Guidebook* series with other valuable life lessons.

Table of Contents

DISCLAIMER: I do not pretend to be a financial guru. In fact, I have absolutely no formal education in finance. I have, however, read a lot of books about finance. Not a day goes by where I am not reading and learning more about personal finance, the stock market, or the economy. I have made every effort to make all of the following information as accurate as can be. In the end, make your own financial decisions and be responsible for them.

INTRODUCTION

"Congratulations! Today is YOUR day, you're off to great places, you're off and away!" Dr. Seuss

No, really. Congratulations! You have taken the first step to investing in your future by reading this!

Let's begin with knowing the difference between *saving* and *investing*.
- Saving is preventing the loss of the money you work for.
- Investing is allowing your money to work for you.

Investing and financial management may seem to be a daunting task at first, but it doesn't have to be. You may think the stock market is risky, and it certainly can be. But you have the power to control your level of risk. The stock market is a powerful way to obtain wealth, even while you're sleeping. Don't be afraid of it, be informed.

Saving probably sounds boring to you right now, especially saving for retirement. The fact of the matter is that you cannot create wealth without saving. Stop playing the short game and start to think long term. I realize that thinking far ahead is a difficult thing to do, and maybe not very fun. Not being able to afford a home, a car, medications, or food is also not very fun. Remember, a long journey starts with a single step. So let's take that first step and focus on your goals.

Step 1: What are your goals?

- Go to college? Live in a big house? Have a family? Travel? Be wealthy? Before you read any further, write down at least 5 goals you have.

Step 2: What annual salary do you want?

- If you don't have a target in mind, you won't know if you reached it. If you shoot low, you will remain low. Set an optimistic target. Write it down now.

Step 3: What do you like to do?

- In other words, what is something you could do for free, or even lose money doing, and still have fun? Don't think about how to earn money with this yet, it's just to get you thinking. Write down at least 5 things that fit this criteria. If you can't think of any, then get out of your comfort zone and experiment with new experiences.

Step 4: Let's go!

When some 90+ year old people were interviewed and asked about regrets in their life, some of their top answers were that they **worried too much** and they **didn't take enough risks**.

Finances can be an incredible source of worry for a lot of people. **Investing should not add more worry, but should actually take some of it away by knowing that you are investing in your future.**

There will be risks along the way, and you will lose some money, perhaps more than what you're comfortable with. Some of the nation's top investors will easily tell you **they have learned more from their losses and mistakes than from their successes**. The best investors can use their mistakes and losses to their advantage by adjusting their investing behavior accordingly, and not making that mistake again.

You may not realize it, but you are an investor right now. The fact that you are reading this means that you are investing your time in hopes that it will provide some sort of return. When you set your alarm clock in the morning, you are balancing the benefit of sleep with the amount of stress you are willing to tolerate in the morning to get to school or work. When you eat, you may be more willing to make short-term benefits over long-term detriment. See? You are actually an investor already!

Do you feel like you are just keeping your head above water? Do you feel stressed by your constant lack of time? That is a big red flag for failure to self-manage. If you cannot manage your daily investment in your time or health, then you have a good place to start. **Investing daily in good, solid, positive behaviors will spill over its advantages to all aspects of your life.**

CHAPTER 1: HABITS

"Out there things can happen, and frequently do, to people as brainy and footsy as you."
Dr. Seuss

Start some good habits right now. According to several surveys, successful people have these things in common. It's not guaranteed that you will be successful if you do these things, but they will sure help you along the way. They reflect a certain mentality of success. If you want to be successful in managing your life, then set table with these habits:

1) Wake up early. The most productive time of the day is the first few hours.
2) Exercise daily. Physical health does wonders for mental health and optimism.
3) Eat healthy (especially breakfast). Physical and mental health depends on nutrition.
4) Make a list and do the hardest task first. The rest of the day will feel much easier.
5) Be willing to work hard and put in the extra hours needed. Don't trust in luck.
6) Make your bed every morning. It creates an immediate sense of task accomplishment.
7) Reduce the clutter. If you work in a mess, your mind tends to stray and lose focus.
8) Check email only twice a day. Don't let your email dictate your life.
9) Get your face out of your phone. Look up and around, interact, don't miss life.
10) If you need creativity, devote 4 or 5 hours on the task. Don't rush it.

In the book *World Changes*, by John Byrne, he interviews 25 entrepreneurs who changed the face of business. After reading this book, I can say that all of those entrepreneurs worked harder than anybody I have ever known. Sunrise to sunset, 24/7. These entrepreneurs were so focused on their ventures, that they could not physically live without them. It consumed them and ran deep down to the marrow of their bones. Many failed, were fired, or went bankrupt, but none lost hope and all used these obstacles as life lessons. In fact, many of these successful businesses wouldn't exist if it wasn't for those inopportune twists of fate. Looking back, these entrepreneurs were able to connect the dots in their lives that lead them to success. More on that later.

Your attitude can lift you, or hold you down. Successful people have a particular attitude, summarized by the following:

1) **When bad things happen, don't throw your hands up in the air and act helpless.** It may not be fair. Many things in life are not fair. View these as obstacles to overcome, and learn lessons from them. I saw a play once where an actor looked to the sky and dramatically whined "Maybe we should just give up!" It was comedic at the moment, but how many times have you mentally thought or acted like this?
2) **Be confident in yourself and your abilities.** Believe that you have a purpose, because you do. You may not know what you are good at, or what you even like to do, but be confident that you will find it one day.
3) **Be an advocate for yourself, but don't think you're better or smarter than others.** Remember that you can always learn something from anyone. Be humble.
4) **If you want something done, take the initiative and get it done.** Don't just complain about it or wait around for others to do it. Make it a habit that you can only complain about something if you have some plausible solutions in mind and are willing to take action.

5) **There usually are no easy answers, so stop looking for them.**
6) **Chose a direction and go with it**, but don't be afraid or so stuck in your ways where you can't change course along the way. Indecisiveness is weakness. If you are truly having difficulty making a decision, mentally make one, then see how you feel about it for a day or two. If you feel at peace with your decision, then go for it. On the other hand, sticking with a poor decision after you realize it was wrong is just stubbornness.
7) **Be respectful to others**, you never know who you will meet someday.
8) **Don't burning bridges.** It can be one of the worst mistakes you can make.
9) **Don't think you can do it all yourself.** Connect yourself with people at 3 different levels.
    a) The first level is someone who can act as a mentor to you. This should be someone who you admire or hope to emulate. Step out of your comfort zone and reach out. Many people at the top of their fields can be surprisingly easy to reach (with enough persistence).
    b) The second level is someone who is on the same level as you. This is a friend you can share things with, and hold each other accountable.
    c) The third level is someone whom you can be a mentor to. This is someone who may be disadvantaged in some way, or someone looking for a mentor. You can still learn from this person. Acting as an example for someone also helps keep you accountable.

In the book *How To Get Filthy Rich in Rising Asia*, by Mohsin Hamid, he writes a very interesting story and summarizes what he thinks are key attributes to a very successful (and rich) entrepreneur. Not just a little rich, but filthy rich. These are my takeaways from this book:

- Live where the action is for your particular venture or interest. (Ex: Silicon Valley, San Francisco, L.A., New York, etc.)
- Get an education. You can educate yourself with books and with mentors if you're motivated enough. Mark Zuckerberg has stated that he learned more from his hobbies than by a formal education.
- Don't fall in love early on. You don't have the time and you need to stay focused when starting out.
- Be cautious of academics. They are quick to dictate what you should be doing when many of them haven't done those things themselves.
- Find a mentor and attach yourself to them. This is perhaps the number one thing you can do to slingshot yourself to where you want to be. Not just any mentor, but a master of what you want to do.
- Work for yourself. You can get rich working for others, but you can get filthy rich working for yourself.
- Do not be violent, but know there is great evil in this world. Don't be a weakling. As Theodore Roosevelt once said, "Speak softly, and carry a big stick."
- A bureaucratic friend can cut the red tape and push you ahead of the herd.
- Don't leverage your own money. Leverage other people's money.
- Focus on the fundamentals by cutting costs, hiring the right people, and working hard.
- Have an exit strategy and keep an eye on the big picture. Think 30 years in advance.

CHAPTER 2: DISCIPLINE

The current day foremost authority on discipline is Jocko Willink. He is a decorated Navy SEAL who founded the company Echelon Front, which offers leadership training to other companies. Want to get a handle on discipline? Then listen to Jocko's podcast. He is a living example of discipline and has the ability to articulate practical advice and life lessons, learned from his military experiences, from books, and from history. This podcast has the power to literally change your life and put you on a positive, powerful trajectory.

Jocko Willink wrote the book *Extreme Ownership*, with Leif Babin. Get it, read it, and use a highlighter. His coined phrase is "Discipline Equals Freedom." If you are able to maintain discipline in your daily life, you inoculate yourself and become more resistant to problems stemming from lack of motivation, fatigue, or deficits in mental and physical wellbeing.

- Will you be problem free? Of course not.
- Will you learn how to handle these problems better? Yes.
- Will you learn how to lead others to do the same? Yes.
- Does this have the power to improve your life and make you better? You bet.

Discipline is the cornerstone needed to obtain a positive trajectory in life. If you want to obtain happiness, be disciplined. If you want to obtain and maintain wealth, be disciplined.

As Jocko says, if you find that you lack discipline, then you haven't made the decision to be disciplined yet. **Discipline comes from deep within. It is a decision you have to make.** You either are, or aren't. So, are you ready to make the decision to be disciplined? Are you willing to get up early when you don't feel like it? Are you willing to eat right when someone brings free donuts to work? Can you push through fatigue and exercise? With discipline, comes freedom. Freedom from being a slave to your emotions or negative habits. **As certain as the sun coming up tomorrow, you will not be successful without discipline.**

CHAPTER 3: CONNECTING THE DOTS

Listen to the commencement address of Steve Jobs to the 2005 graduates of Stanford. He artfully outlines how to pursue your dreams and live life to the fullest. He also talks about the importance of **connecting the dots in life**. Steve Jobs dropped out of college, allowing him to skip the required prerequisite classes and take only the classes he enjoyed. Taking a calligraphy class didn't make sense at the time, but later it proved to have a profound impact. The following is an excerpt from the speech:

"None of this had even a hope of any practical application in my life. But 10 years later, when we were designing the first Macintosh computer, it all came back to me. And we designed it all into the Mac. It was the first computer with beautiful typography. If I had never dropped in on that single course in college, the Mac would have never had multiple typefaces or proportionally spaced fonts. And since Windows just copied the Mac, it's likely that no personal computer would have them. If I had never dropped out, I would have never dropped in on this calligraphy class, and personal computers might not have the wonderful typography that they do. Of course it was impossible to connect the dots looking forward when I was in college. But it was very, very clear looking backwards 10 years later." - Steve Jobs

CHAPTER 4: I JUST WANT TO BE HAPPY

So why is making money important? We know that money doesn't bring you happiness, otherwise all the lottery winners, celebrities and professional athletes would be the happiest people in the world. Money doesn't make you happy, but **money gives you choices. It is those choices that can bring happiness.** With money, you will feel more in control of your life. Without money, you severely limit your choices and ultimately feel like you are dealing with one curveball after another, playing life on the defensive. Take life by the horns and get control of your situation.

If you choose an hourly wage, you choose your salary based on time. That's fine if you want a 9 to 5 job. If, however, you choose to be self-employed, or have a commission based salary, you base your salary on results. **There is no shortage of money in the world, only a shortage of people willing to work hard and invest in themselves.** As you become older, you begin to realize that time is one of the most valuable things in life. Work smarter with the time that you have.

CHAPTER 5: SPENDING

So where to start? If you are in your teens, you are likely living at home with your parents providing a great deal of your needs. Use this time to focus on creating good financial habits and developing discipline. **Perhaps one of the most effective ways to get a hold of your finances is to live frugally and stop the leaks.** This means to live below your means. Easier said than done.

Living on 50% of your income is a good benchmark for living frugally. In fact, saving 50% of your income will provide you with massive freedom. This takes a certain disciplined mindset to accomplish. It's a way of life, much like exercise and eating healthy. Even if you have a minimum wage job, get in the habit of saving half. Examples of living frugally are: use a flip phone (laughing? Billionaire Warren Buffett uses a flip phone), make your own coffee, cut coupons, buy food in bulk when it's on sale, drive an old car and run it into the ground, turn down the thermostat in the winter, cycle the AC in the summer (or don't even have air conditioning), don't have cable, live in a house with a mortgage of less than 20% of your income, and for goodness sake, only use a credit card to the extent you can pay it off every month!

Recurring monthly expenses are like death by a thousand papercuts. Avoid them at all costs. Do you really need to subscribe to hundreds of channels? Do you need that monthly gym membership? You can get ripped with calisthenics and all you need is gravity, which is free here on Earth. You think I'm joking? Check out *ThenX* (short for calisthenics) on YouTube and get started.

Simplify your life. You can do this as a teenager by not accumulating junk. Most people have hundreds or thousands of dollars worth of stuff lying around that could be sold or donated (don't forget to take the tax deduction). Go through your stuff at least every 6 months. If you haven't touched it in the last 6 months, get rid of it.

Think twice before buying things. It's a good idea to ask yourself the following questions:
1) **Is this something that will last?** If you're going to buy something, don't buy cheap garbage that will break or prematurely wear out.
2) **Will this bring me happiness?** If it's short lived happiness, maybe you'll be just fine without it. Will a new car bring you significantly more happiness than a used car?

Don't get me wrong, it is very important to have hobbies and spend a little on vacations, experiences, and toys. Budget for them and be wise about where your money goes. Short lived purchases do not add up to long term happiness. When I recall what I have spent money on over the years, it is *experiences,* rather than items, that tend to bring me greater happiness. So remember this, before you buy things, you would be wise to first pause and reflect a moment as to what is truly important to you.

Be keenly aware of advertising. Entire professions and vast sums of money are spent on designing methods to entice you to spend more. Sales, discounts, and deals easily lure you to spend. There are even psychological tricks, which you aren't even aware of, that are being used on you. It is truly a physical and psychological war and unless you are able to maintain discipline with your spending, you will lose.

During your initial years, **you need money to make money**. So how do you get money? You work! You can't make a snowman without starting with a snowball. Saving more money is, in a sense, paying yourself additional income. Try not having a car. You save on the purchase, interest, registration, taxes, gas, insurance, and maintenance. Try biking or taking public transportation instead. Sure it may be inconvenient at times, but so is being broke. Bottom line is that **if you want to fill a tub with water, plugging up the drain is the first place to start.**

It may surprise you, but you wouldn't know a majority of millionaires in the United States if you saw them on the street or drove by their house. There's a book written called *The Millionaire Next Door*, by Thomas Stanley and William Danko, that describes this phenomenon. A majority of millionaires live in houses less than $400,000 and are more likely to drive an old car than a BMW. **A majority of wealthy Americans get wealthy by living below their means.** They are not dependent on the government or their relatives. What was found is that a majority of those who are flashy with their money live well above their means and are in debt up to their ears. **It's time to start acting like a millionaire and live frugally!**

CHAPTER 6: BUDGETING

To budget means to create a set of financial guidelines to live by. Money coming in should be more than money going out. Simple enough, right?

Some general guidelines to distribute your income are as follows:

- 50% Savings and Investing
- 15% Housing and Insurance
- 10% Donations
- 10% Utilities: phone, heat, water, internet
- 5% Transportation: bike, car, bus, maintenance
- 5% Groceries
- 5% Misc: travel, fun, books, gym, etc.

You may be surprised at some of these percentages. Each person's situation is a bit different and some of these percentages may change. The number one percentage to adhere to is saving and investing 50% of your income. Everything else can be made to work. Will it be hard? Yes. You can roll over and say it is not possible, or you can use it as an opportunity to develop some discipline in your life.

To help make your budget work, increase your income and decrease your spending. Simple as that. Years ago, I was having a tough time making ends meet. Money, or lack of, became a huge stressor in my life. Like a switch, I decided right then and there that I was going to make more money and decrease my spending. It wasn't an option. I just got to it, made some sacrifices, worked harder, and did it. You can do it if you commit to it.

Why donate 10%? **Someone will always have it worse than you.** It is a surprising fact that as income goes up, donations generally go down. There are some unfortunate circumstances in life that just happen to good people. Through no fault of their own, they are left in a dire situation. You might be one of those people one day. Start now and commit to helping others.

CHAPTER 7: BORROWING

It is inevitable that at some time in your life, you will need to borrow some money. Borrowing is not always a bad thing. Borrowing allows you to buy and do things now, and pay for them sometime further down the road. Borrowing, if used properly, can allow you to get an education, to move to where the action is, or to get your foot in the door. Borrowing, if done correctly, can slingshot your way to success.

Borrowing creates debt. Don't be afraid of some debt. There's good debt, and there's bad debt. Good debt is tax deductible, low interest, can be used to establish credit, and is used to further your career. Credit is a measure of how reliable you are at paying off a debt. If you never pay back your debt, nobody will want to lend you money. Common sense, right? This is expressed by a number called your credit score.

Credit is when you borrow money and are charged a fee for using that money, such as a credit card. That fee is called interest. The interest is commonly referred to as APR, or annual percentage rate. It is the percentage of your loan that you will pay annually. The lower the APR, the lower your monthly payments will be. This is how banks make money. They lend money and charge a fee for using that money.

Keep in mind that APR can change, based on changes in the market. Many banks or lenders will try to lure you with gimmicky low APR offers. Here's how to weed through the thick of it:

First, let's start with the Prime Rate. The Prime Rate is the average of all the interest rates the largest banks charge each other for lending between banks. This rate is published in the Wall Street

Journal daily. This Prime Rate is what banks charge their best customers to borrow money. It usually is between 6 to 10%.

Credit card interest rates are expressed in "Prime + X%". A credit card company may say 5% APR, but it may really mean Prime + 5%. If Prime is 5%, and APR is 5%, then your total interest rate would be 10%. Other companies may express the APR to include Prime. Read the fine print.

A "Fixed APR" rate is a rate that doesn't change, unless the lender decides to change it. It usually does not change on a daily basis and typically remains stable, but it's important to remember that the lender can change it at any time. If interest rates are going up, then look for a loan with a fixed APR.

A "Variable APR" rate is a rate that is tied to some other index. If interest rates are going down, then a variable APR loan is best.

Watch out for teaser rates. These are special rates that may be low, but carry stiff penalties if the attached limitations are broken. A few late payments and you could be looking at a 30% penalty. There also may be other hidden fees. Again, read the fine print, it's there for a reason.

Auto loans and mortgages are calculated a bit different. As you pay down the principal, the less interest your monthly payment will be. This process of making a monthly payment over a fixed time is called amortization.

If you never have any debt, no one will ever know if you can pay off a debt. It is for this reason that having some debt can actually help your credit score. For example, a credit card can show that you are good for the money, as long as you pay off the entire balance monthly. If you can pay the entire balance off monthly, you will never get charged interest.

Examples of good debt includes a house, or student loans. Make the payments on time and your credit score will remain solid. So why do I need a good credit score? Someday, you may want to borrow some money to get a business off the ground, to expand some real estate, or to make an investment. **Leveraging other people's money can be a great way to build wealth, and it may all come down to your credit score.**

Avoid bad debt! Bad debt is high interest debt that harms your credit score, such as credit card debt, or high priced auto loans. **Bad debt is like a hole you dig yourself into**. Once in that hole, it is very difficult to escape. Harmful effects of bad debt will ripple throughout your entire life. Dings on your credit can make it difficult to get into a house or obtain any other financing. Avoid bad debt at all costs!

As a general rule, avoid debt that doesn't serve a long-term purpose to furthering yourself, your career, or your wealth creating potential. If you cannot make your debt payments on time, every time, then you should not have that debt.

You might be thinking, "I work at a minimum wage job with no benefits. I can't begin to think about paying for a car, or college, much less save for retirement! How is this all possible?" Well, it is possible. Let's dive right in.

CHAPTER 8: THE POWER OF TIME

You have an Ace up your sleeve. You may not even realize it, but you have an Ace that not even some of the most powerful investors have. Many successful investors have stated that they would be **willing to give up everything** they have earned in order to have the Ace that you have. What is that Ace? **Time.**

Time is perhaps the strongest factor in investing. One reason for this is compound growth. What is compound growth? Another way to say it is growth on growth. Let's say you invested $100 and earned an interest rate of 10%. What is an interest rate, you ask? Interest rate is money paid at a certain time for the benefit of using that money. At a rate of 10%, after 1 year, you would have $110. Simple enough. The next year, the base is $110 instead of $100. So instead of gaining by just $10 per year, you gain at $11, so now you have $121. The next year, you gain by $12.10, so now you have $133.10. **It is growth on growth.**

Some stocks will pay a dividend, which is a small cut of the business's profits. If this dividend is automatically reinvested, it adds perpetually to the quantity of stock you own in that company, thus feeding the compound growth cycle. Think of it like a small stone that starts an avalanche. One stone rolls and hits another stone, which both hit more stones, and soon an avalanche develops. Picture those stones being dollars.

Enter in the **Rule of 72**. This is a simple calculation used to determine how long it will take to double your money, given a fixed compound annual interest rate. Divide 72 by the percent compound interest rate, and you'll get the number of years. For example, if you have a compound annual interest rate of 6%, then 72/6 = 12 years. So if you invest $1000 and let it sit for 12 years in a low cost index fund, and don't touch it, it will become $2000.

The power of compound growth can be thought of in a different way as well. Think of that extra $10 in your pocket as a small stone. You may want to spend it now on some egg rolls, but that small stone could be the starting stone of an avalanche. If you invest it now, it will undergo compound growth and be worth much more several years from now. Once you realize that, you will look at that $10 very differently. Invest for long term gain, rather than spend it for short term rewards. This goes back to the disciplined mindset. Your will is stronger than an egg roll.

So how can you use compound growth right now? **Go out and open a Roth IRA right now (as long as you have earned income)!** You might have heard that a Roth IRA is used to save for retirement, which is true, but it has more benefits. Here are some key advantages of a Roth IRA:

1) The Roth is not included on the FAFSA (Free Application for Federal Student Aid), so it does not count against you for obtaining financial aid.
2) You can use your **contributions** towards education, as long as you have had it open for at least 5 years. You can use the **earnings** as well, but at a 10% penalty.
3) You can use the principal of your Roth IRA towards the purchase of your first home if you want, to a maximum of $10,000.
4) Drawing from a Roth IRA after age 59 ½ is TAX FREE!
5) Your contributions to a Roth can be taken out and used for emergencies at any time.

As long as you earn an income, open a Roth IRA! Ok, so if I open a Roth and put money in, how does it grow? Make it an investment account and buy stocks. More on that later.

CHAPTER 9: COLLEGE

"Think left and think right and think low and think high. Oh, the thinks you can think up if only you try!" Dr. Seuss

College, or no college? It's true that you can certainly succeed if you have the motivation, the drive, and the maturity, by not going to college. You can learn by teaching yourself, with online classes, or with finding a mentor or apprenticeship. Before you blow off college, think about your life's goals. It is very difficult to go back to school once you decide not to. If you do not have a formal higher education, you will never be a medical professional. You will also never become a lawyer, a dentist, a veterinarian, a teacher, and the list goes on. Some professions absolutely require a higher degree. With so many applicants, many employers won't even look at you unless you have a degree. Don't take this decision lightly.

Having a higher education is a tool that can help propel your career to ultimately earn a higher income. Taking on education debt needs to be balanced with what income you expect to make with that degree. Recall from Steve Job's commencement speech, however, that he didn't even realize at the time the importance of some classes he took. You cannot know all of the facts right now. Life's goals change. What you can know, is that more education never hurts. If in doubt, go to college and embrace it as an opportunity to further yourself, both in maturity and knowledge.

How do you pay for the cost of college? If you're still a teenager, you can **obtain college credits while still in high school.** If you are mature enough and are comfortable taking classes with students a bit older than you, you can potentially save half, or even a full year, of tuition expenses. Search for *smaller* community colleges to fulfill these to credits. Smaller colleges allow you to individualize classes better and can reduce the social pressure of a larger college.

Starting at least three years before college, **search for grants and scholarships**. There are some lesser known grants and scholarships that you may be able to tailor your class schedule to earn. There is money out there, you just have to find it.

Obviously, apply with the FAFSA and see what you can get. It is a myth that students do not get financial aid if their parents make too much money. You must apply with the FAFSA.

There are many books that outline how to exactly pay for college. All methods require planning by you, some as early as 7th grade. There are methods that work, but all require effort.

Student debt is not necessarily a bad thing. It is tax deductible and helps your credit, as long as you make all of your payments on time. Automate your payments to ensure they are always on time. You typically can get a reduced interest rate with automated payments, so be sure to ask. Consolidating your student debt can also help reduce your interest rates. Colleges have financial guidance professionals to help walk you through this process. Don't fully rely on them, however. Do your own research as well.

Bachelor of Arts, or Bachelor of Sciences? You will find that many employers now look for well-rounded individuals who have unique problem solving skills, who are well versed in a variety of topics, who are able to maintain a sense of balance in their lives, and who show appreciation for art, culture, literature, and the environment around them. Choose a variety of classes to get a taste of what is out there. **Follow your passion, but don't neglect dabbling in unfamiliar territory.** It can be equally as valuable to learn what you don't like, than it is to learn what you do.

A word about literature. Being able to communicate an idea in a concise and clear manner can make or break the best idea, strategy, discovery or creation. You may have the best idea in the world, but it means nothing if you cannot adequately communicate it. **Words have meaning and words have power.** In fact, wars are prevented, or created, with words. You won't grow in your communication skills until you begin to study and analyze literature, or until you are graded and your words are picked apart by someone who is a master with words. Whatever you do, take at least some classes in literature and read quality material.

Before you decide what career path you will pursue, read the book *The Four Hour Work Week*, by Tim Ferriss. It may completely change your perspective on your life's goals and how to get there. He also has great insight with his podcasts, which focuses on picking apart the habits and tools of successful people. In fact, it's one of the few podcasts I will consistently listen to. You won't regret it.

CHAPTER 10: MULTIPLE INCOME STREAMS

You've heard of not putting all your eggs in one basket. When choosing a career path, keep in mind that it is a good idea to have multiple options with that career. Your likes and dislikes may change, the economy may shift, new technology may emerge or displace you, and your life's goals or economic status may change. Having a career with flexibility is one way to safeguard your future.

One of the greatest advice tips from millionaires and billionaires is to **have multiple income streams related to your field**. For instance, if you're a health professional, you can have a clinical job, a managerial role, a consulting side-business, be an author, be a researcher, and have an online presence. If one stream dries up or fails, you are not left high and dry.

The key is having streams related to your field. That is your niche and your area of expertise. For example, if you're a doctor, don't open a coffee shop just because you enjoy coffee.

"Simple it's not, I'm afraid you will find, for a mind maker-upper to make up his mind." Dr. Seuss

Bottom line is that **a diverse educational background can help you create, develop, and succeed with multiple streams of income.** Keep this in mind when considering your college path.

This isn't to say you should pursue several different income streams simultaneously. As Tim Ferriss reminds us with Buridan's fable, **don't be a donkey**. Picture a donkey that is standing halfway between water and hay. He's hungry and he's thirsty, but doesn't know which direction to go first. The donkey ends up dying of dehydration and hunger. Don't be a donkey and travel a millimeter in all directions, only to end up nowhere.

CHAPTER 11: INSURANCE

Risk is unavoidable. A simple accident can cost you your hard earned savings. Insurance is a way to mitigate the risk of financial fallout due to accidents or theft. As you get older, have more wealth to protect, and have people dependent on you, your need for insurance increases.

There are several types of insurance. Until you are off on your own, you are typically protected under your parent's insurance. Once you turn 18, it is time to think about the following types of insurance:
- Renters: Provides coverage for losses related to theft, fire, vandalism, and liability in case a visitor gets injured.
- Auto: Provides coverage for accidents, liability, and roadside assistance in some cases.
- Health: Provides coverage for medical bills and prescriptions.

As with all insurance, you generally get what you pay for. There is cheap insurance that doesn't cover a whole lot, and there is more expensive insurance with broader coverage. Shop around for insurance to get the best value of both rates *and* coverage. Don't shop around from one insurance company to another. You will be better served by being loyal if you ever need to make a claim. Many insurance companies will offer multi-line discounts if you have more than one type of insurance with them.

There is some terminology to become familiar with when dealing with insurance.

- Insurance Premium: This is the amount you pay to have the insurance. It can be paid monthly, quarterly, semiannually, or annually. Some companies offer discounts if paid annually. The premium gets higher with the more coverage you have. Pay with credit card if you can, to help build reward points.
- Deductible: This is the amount you pay up front when you are making a claim. The higher the deductible, the lower your premium will be. It's a tradeoff. Are you more comfortable with a higher upfront cost (deductible) or a cost that is distributed over time (premium)?
- Copayment: This refers to health insurance. It's a fixed amount you pay for receiving a health service. This copayment is above what insurance covers.

As you get older and start to build more wealth, have a house, have dependents, and a steady salary, there are many other types of insurance that begin to come into play. Namely, homeowners insurance, life insurance, and disability insurance.

Many people have inadequate disability coverage, even though it is much more likely to become disabled than it is to die unexpectedly. Many employers offer some sort of disability insurance, but be sure to get coverage outside of your employer as well. Why? For two big reasons:

1) If you become disabled, disbursements from employer sponsored disability plans typically are taxed, whereas your own disability coverage is not.
2) Employer disability plans typically cover only a fraction of your actual salary, leaving you grossly under covered

if you become disabled. Having both an employer plan, and your own plan, can provide adequate coverage.

If you get in an accident and become disabled where you cannot work your current job, the last thing you want is to become a burden for your family and have to dramatically change your lifestyle to make ends meet. It is your responsibility to your family to make sure you are covered.

So what about life insurance? When you're young and healthy (hopefully), the best life insurance to get is term. This means that you have a fixed monthly premium for the term of the insurance (10, 20, or 30 years), even if your health changes during that time. It's important to know that term life insurance is temporary and does not accumulate any cash value.

Permanent life insurance is very different than term. Whole life insurance is an example of a permanent policy. These typically involve much larger monthly premiums, but they are permanent and actually have a cash value. There are certainly some situations where whole life makes sense, such as with estate planning or if you have a lifelong dependent.

Many people use the phrase "**buy term and invest the difference**". If life insurance companies make money by investing your premium, why not buy cheaper term, save the difference, and invest it yourself? Each person's situation is different, so do your own homework on this subject if you are really considering a permanent policy.

When getting life insurance, be sure to have coverage through when your kids are done with college. If you happen to die while your kids are in college and you don't have coverage, they may have to drop out due to a sudden loss of finances. If you have a 10 or 20 year term plan, you can renew your policy for an additional 20 years, say when you're getting close to 40 years old, as long as you are still healthy at that time.

How much life insurance coverage should you get? A general rule of thumb is to get coverage for at least 10x your annual income. Sounds excessive, but it's really not. You do not want to leave your family high and dry with a mortgage, loans, college costs, medical bills, and funeral expenses.

Homeowners insurance is a must when buying a home. Be sure to review your policy and make sure it accurately represents your house. It pays to review your policy after major home improvements or remodeling. Oftentimes, homeowners insurance is wrapped up in escrow, meaning the bank collects a portion of your premium with every mortgage payment, then pays the insurance company when the policy comes due. It is a nice way to distribute insurance payments with each house payment and ensures coverage at all times.

It pays to have your Homeowners, Auto, Life, etc. under one roof, by a big reputable company, such as State Farm. With all of it under one roof, you can get a multi-line discount and can speak with an agent to ensure adequate coverage across the board.

CHAPTER 12: HOUSING

Where you live can be one of the most important decisions you can make. **If you want to propel your career, live where the action is.** For example, if you want to make movies, you likely won't get far living in rural Wisconsin. If you're into fashion, you should choose New York over North Dakota. Get what I'm saying?

On the other hand, realize that **family is important**. You may be young and feel free as a bird, but don't sever ties with your family. If you are going to have a family yourself one day, living by family and having a strong support network will help maintain sanity. One of the biggest factors of longevity is having a strong sense of community and a support network of friends and family.

What if family and career goals don't coincide? Quoting Hamlet, "There lies the rub." **In all things, there is sacrifice and there are compromises.**

So you've chosen what city you are going to live in. Great. Now, where do you live in that city? You've heard the phrase, "**Location, location, location.**" What does that mean? A house in a desirable area will maintain great resale value and increase in value disproportionately more than those in undesirable areas. That sounds like a good investment to me. Living close to work means a shorter commute, which tends to be one of the most stressful times of the day. Do yourself a favor and eliminate the commute. Choose where to live based on ease of transportation. Being able to bike or walk to work serves many purposes by saving time and money, creating exercise, reducing stress, and toughening you up.

Rent or own? It depends on your situation. In general, do whatever you can to own. It is almost always the better route to go (unless you can predict an upcoming housing crisis). "I'm not sure I'm going to stay here." you say. Guess what? If you rent, you still sign a lease agreement. Renting may seem easier, but if you rent, you have nothing to show for it at the end of your stay. All that money, gone.

Here's a trick to make owning happen. Buy a house and rent the rooms to classmates or coworkers to offset the mortgage. Don't have money for a down payment on a house? Talk to a mortgage specialist for ideas. Get a parent to cosign. Worried about costly repairs? Work a home warranty into the purchase agreement. There are ways to get into a house and make it work. When it comes time to move, you have built equity and the house, it has hopefully increased in value, and your renters have helped offset the mortgage. Your home becomes your investment and you've just leveraged other people's money (the bank) to make money. That's an awesome trick.

Pay your house off early. A mortgage is made up of principal and interest. Although your interest rate may be low, and tax deductible, you are paying an incredible amount of money in interest alone. **If you pay your principal and interest, but then also pay the principal for the next month, you will end up paying your house off in half the time and save tens of thousands of dollars!** Get a 30 year mortgage, but pay it off in 15 years using this method. Why not just get a 15 year mortgage with a lower interest rate? Because that forces you into a higher payment and if you can't make that payment, you lose the house. By getting a 30 year mortgage, you have the option to pay it off early, but don't get penalized if you can't make those extra payments, such as in the case of a financial emergency.

You can also use this method to calculate what size of house you can afford. For example, if you have a 3 bedroom house and plan on renting 2 of the rooms at $600/month each, that gives you a monthly income of $1200. If you're looking at a house and calculate your monthly mortgage as $1000 (principal payment of $400 +

interest of $600), you will want to ideally pay the principal for the next month as well. Your monthly payment would then be $400 + $400 + $600, which is $1400. If you rent out 2 rooms for $1200, you end up paying just $200/mo. to live in the house yourself, with the advantage of building equity. This is an example of **using other people's money as leverage for your investment**. Of course, with a 30 year mortgage, you don't have to pay the next month's principal. You could pay just the $1000/mo. mortgage, and use the extra $200/mo. towards home improvements, utilities, contributing to savings, etc.

With all of this being said, **do not buy a house you can afford**. **Buy a house that is LESS than what you can afford.** Take the excess and invest. Remember the millionaire next door? You do not want to tie yourself to a big house payment. Jobs change, family needs change, and other situations arise. With a big house comes big bills with repairs, heating and cooling, insurance, etc. Focus on what you really need, not what you really want.   There is a lot to be said about having kids share bedrooms. Having a big house means that people spread out more. This is the first step in creating an environment where family becomes more distant, where people spend more time on their phones than with each other, or just don't even know what their kids are up to. If you physically have less space, this becomes harder to do. Learning to share and living with less are valuable life lessons you can bestow on your kids, just by buying a smaller house.

Some people say, "Do NOT pay your house off early." They state the following reasons:
- Mortgage interest isn't that bad because it decreases over time. As you pay down your principal, the amount of interest you pay also decreases.
- Invested dollars grow at roughly 9% annually. If your mortgage interest is 4%, you can make more money by investing rather than paying off your mortgage early.

- Invested dollars grow compound, ultimately leading to more than a 9% growth annually. Once you pay down your mortgage, that money is gone forever.
- Mortgage interest is also tax deductible, reducing your tax burden.

Although all of these things are true, here is the flip side:
- Your job may not remain reliable and your income stream could suddenly change. If you pay your house off early, you won't have the fear of having to move unexpectedly.
- Although invested dollars grow at roughly 9% annually, there are certainly times when the market underperforms for several years in a row. You do not want to be in a situation where you need to sell stock in a down market.
- The advantages of not paying down your mortgage early is only realized if you are disciplined enough to invest that amount. How many of us have "extra" money laying around? Either you automate paying your mortgage down early, or you automate your investing. It rarely works to rely on "paying what you can" if you have a little extra that month. If you aren't disciplined enough to invest, then paying down your mortgage is a guaranteed way to save money.
- There are psychological benefits of getting rid of housing debt. There is a feeling of freedom and financial security when you are able to live in a house without a mortgage. Your house becomes a place you call home and unless you declare bankruptcy due to other debt, no one can take that away from you.

CHAPTER 13: EMPLOYMENT

"If things start happening, don't worry, don't stew, just go right along, and you'll start happening too." Dr. Seuss

Treat every job as an opportunity to learn. Whether it's stocking shelves, talking with customers, or washing dishes, you can find something to learn from any job. Having said that, choose jobs that can act as stepping stones to where you want to go.

Lead where you are. If you're not part of management and don't have the power to change things, all is not lost. If fact, consider it a challenge and be thankful for the opportunity to show your worth. Come up with ideas, dial them in, and present them. Lead your co-workers, provide for them, take responsibility for your team's failures, and deflect compliments back to your teammates. When the time comes to have a leader, guess who's getting chosen?

The way you carry yourself at work and in public can deeply influence how people treat you, and how you perceive yourself. It can make or break opportunities. Heed these simple tips to become a power figure:

- **Posture:** Stand and sit up straight. Don't slouch in a chair. Having good posture exudes confidence and a sense of trust. It's good for you, too.
- **Eye contact:** Look at who is talking in the eye. Keep and maintain strong eye contact. It tells the person they are important and worth listening to. It creates the feeling that you actually care. Strong eye contact also signals a sense of confidence.
- **Clothing:** If you dress like crap, people will treat you like crap. Never be the worst dressed person in the room. If you

look good, you feel good. If you feel good, your attitude is lifted and you become more positive. People are naturally drawn to that and want to spend time with a positive person. If you dress like a mature adult, more responsibility will be given to you.

- **Speech:** Speak loud enough to be heard, but don't be boisterous. Enunciate your words. Hold your chin up, sit up straight, and say what you mean to say with confidence. Be a wordsmith and choose your words carefully. Be descriptive and informative as concisely as possible. Speak to others as you would like them to speak to you. Pay attention to your tone of voice. Be quicker to listen than to speak.

- **Cell phones:** Don't have your cell phone out when talking with people. Don't even have it sitting on the table. Doing so tells that person that you are willing to spend time with them, unless something more important happens, such as getting a text or a call. Trying to hide your phone under the table at a meeting fools no one. Be present.

- **Personal grooming:** Don't smell. Brush your teeth and maintain good hygiene. The more you look the part, the more you will feel the part, and the more you will succeed at the part.   If you can't pay attention to your own grooming, you won't be trusted to pay attention to a business deal.

- **Mimic behavior:** If you mimic someone's behavior, the higher the chance they will associate with you. If they're leaning against the wall, you should too. If they're holding their hands in front of themselves, you should too. Doing so creates a sense of association and comfort, lowering their guard and opens them up to being led by you.

- **Integrity:** Be known as a pinnacle of trustworthiness, loyalty, faith and integrity. The moment you begin to lie, evade, or manipulate is the moment you can never take back. No matter how deserving, do not break down others in attempts to build yourself up.

- **Gossip:** Avoid gossip like the plague. Not only is it wrong, but walls have ears.

CHAPTER 14: WHERE TO STASH THAT CASH

There are three main ways to plan for your financial future. You can marry into money, you can inherit money, or you can start building your own savings. **Stuffing money into a jar won't get you to where you want to be.** With the typical inflation rate of 3%, you are in effect paying 3% a year to keep your money in a jar. When I say a jar, I mean a bank account. Even the best bank savings accounts don't keep up with inflation. Banks use fancy terms such as "High Yield Savings Account" to make you think you are earning a great interest rate, when in reality your rate may be as little as 0.01%. If you want easy accessible cash, say for an emergency fund, a savings bank account is just fine, as long as you **know that you are paying 3% a year to keep it there for the convenience of liquidity and FDIC insurance.** Once you grasp that concept of paying 3% annually, you will be a bit more comfortable with taking on risk.

There are a lot of opinions as to how much money should be kept in an emergency savings account. Some say 6 months of income, but that is unrealistic. **Keep as much cash in the account as necessary to provide you with enough time to liquidate from other sources**. You don't want to sell off stock unless you absolutely have to. It's reasonable to have a good one to two months of income in a savings account. This account should be for emergencies and should rarely be tapped into. If you have to tap into it, replace that amount as quickly as possible. More on this later when we talk about bonds.

How much cash should you have in a safe at home? Think of a number that you would feel uncomfortable with carrying around on the street, then add a zero to it. This will depend on your level of paranoia, but during natural or economic disasters, cash is king.

CHAPTER 15: INVESTMENT VEHICLES

So let's say you entered into a job that offers a 401(k). What should you do? **Once you have established an emergency fund, make sure you have maxed out your 401(k).**

What is a 401(k) anyway? Basically, it's a retirement plan set up by your employer. Once you enroll in it, a portion of your paycheck automatically gets deposited into the 401(k) account. You aren't taxed on that money until you withdraw it during retirement, which is called tax-deferred. This is a huge advantage for the following reasons:

- Once you retire, your income will be much lower, so you'll likely be in a lower tax bracket and ultimately pay less taxes than what you do now.
- Investing pre-tax dollars means a larger chunk of your money starts growing now.
- Your contributions decrease your taxable income, thereby lowering your taxes. Don't pay the government more money than you have to!

Many 401(k) plans limit where you can choose to invest, and many are limited to mutual funds. Ask your employer appointed financial planner for guidance on those specific funds, how to diversify based on your age, your level of risk, and those with the lowest costs.

For added incentive to save, many employers will also contribute to your 401(k), as long as you save a certain percentage of your paycheck. If you don't save at least that amount, you miss out on your employer match and are essentially **throwing free money away!** That is zero risk, guaranteed free money, so take advantage of it!

What kind of funds belong in a 401(k)? Since this is a tax-deferred account, you want tax inefficient funds in your 401(k). This includes corporate or U.S. government bonds, treasury inflation-protected securities (TIPS), and equity index funds.

What are the disadvantages of a 401(k)? The main disadvantages are:

- You have no idea what the tax rate will be when you retire. It could be more than today's current tax rate! Although unlikely that would nullify its primary tax advantage.
- Most employer 401(k) plans offer very limited funds, and nearly all with fees. Your choices are limited and your contributions will likely grow less quickly than your other investments.
- If you leave your employer before you're "fully vested," you cannot take all of your matching funds with you to your next job. It may take several years to become fully vested. This is a method employers use to encourage employee retention.

My advice? The advantages of having a 401(k) vastly outweigh the disadvantages of not having one. Max out your 401(k).

After you've maxed out your 401(k) contributions, look for other tax advantaged ways to save money. If you don't have a Roth IRA yet, open one now! Whereas 401(k) money is taxed at the time of withdrawal, Roth IRA money is taxed before it is invested (contributions are with POST-tax money). Having *both* investment vehicles gives you the best of both worlds. Since you don't know what the tax rate will be in the future, maxing out a Roth IRA now is a smart decision.

In addition to the benefits previously described, the beauty of a Roth IRA is that you have complete control of where, and how, you invest your money. **The Roth IRA is where you will likely have the most stock trades since you do not need to pay taxes on the gains, as long as you don't touch those gains until retirement.**

This allows you to make short term (< 1 year) trades and not get penalized for them.

Many banks or investment firms offer Roth IRAs with a certain number of free trades per year, so you don't even need to pay those fees! Again, like the 401(k), there are penalties for early withdrawal on earnings, so don't plan on touching this money until you retire. Remember, in emergencies, or for education, you can use your contributions (not gains) without penalty. There is an annual contribution limit, so do your best to reach this limit every year. More volatile stocks, index funds, stocks that are frequently traded, and real estate investment trusts all belong in Roth IRA's to capitalize on their tax advantage.

Ok, so you have cash at home, an emergency savings account (you could consider your Roth IRA as a semi-emergency fund), you've maxed out your 401(k), and your Roth IRA. What next? Look for a HSA (health savings account). You may be healthy now, but you will get older and you will need it. **The HSA is one of the most tax-free investment vehicles available.** It's so good, I can't even believe it's legal! It's different than an FSA (flexible savings account) in that it doesn't have the "use it or lose it" annual rule. Although there are some restrictions on who is eligible for an HSA, it is an absolute must have, if you qualify.

So what is an HSA? It's an account that is earmarked for health related expenses. Money contributed is PRE-tax. You can use this money for all qualified medical expenses, such as medical, dental, vision, and prescriptions. The money you don't immediately use can be invested in index or mutual funds. The gains are taxed at the standard income tax level if they are withdrawn after age 65 (tax deferred). They are NOT taxed if used for qualified medical expenses. There is an annual contribution limit, so again, do your best to reach this limit every year.

Looking for additional investment vehicles? Again, permanent life insurance is an option. There are plenty of permanent life insurance options out there, such as variable life and whole life. There are some advantages to these other options, and new insurance vehicles are being developed every year. If you're interested in learning more about some of the new permanent insurance options out there, get advice from an independent source. You wouldn't go to a Toyota dealer and not expect them to tell you how great a Toyota is.

Annuities are a type of insurance product you invest in. In return, you get a steady stream of income later in life. Sounds good, right? Yep, except many annuities have fees of > 2%. My advice is to create your own income stream by focusing on quality dividend paying stocks, and save the fees! Invest in quality companies that have a history of increasing dividends, and rely on the dividends as your income stream. More on this later.

So now what? Your next step is to **start investing in a 529 educational plan**. If you don't have any kids, start one in your own name. A 529 plan allows you to make POST-tax contributions to an investment account that grows tax free, as long as it is used for qualified educational expenses.

Finished with school? Doesn't matter, start one anyway. If you ever have kids who will go to school, then you can transfer the funds to them. What if your kid doesn't go to college? Then transfer it to another kid, or a grandkid! Believe me, they will thank you and it is a tremendous gift to them! Open one early to take advantage of the power of time and compound growth.

A 529 plan is a state sponsored program. Each state has their own benefits and fees. Some states offer additional discounts when their plan is used towards their state's schools. My recommendation is to find a state with the lowest fees and the highest ratings. Alaska and Utah both have extremely good 529 plans.

Why are tax advantaged accounts so important? If you can limit the amount of taxes you pay, you will have more money. Simple as that. Having money in the wrong investment vehicle can tremendously impact your earnings. If you have a choice between two identical cars, but one is 15% off, which would you choose? You may think that your effective tax rate is low right now, but it won't be forever. Plan for increased taxes. **One fact of life is that taxes will always go up.** Everyone has to pay taxes, but you don't need to pay more than your share.

So you've maxed out your tax advantaged accounts. Now what? The next step is to set up a general brokerage account. **This account is not tax advantaged in any way.** This means the investments are made with POST-tax dollars and all profits (capital gains) are also taxed.

Do your best to limit any fees associated with this account. Choose individual stocks, or low cost index funds, rather than mutual funds, to avoid higher mutual fund fees. These fees may not seem like a lot, but they add up and truly diminish your long term compound growth potential. Although some banks offer a certain number of free trades per year, this is getting less common. Many charge a trader commission fee for every trade, so make trades wisely.

What kind of stocks belong in a non-tax advantaged account? General brokerage accounts only hold the stocks, or index funds, that are intended to be long term (> 1 year), in order to avoid the higher short term capital gains taxes. You want to be very careful when choosing these stocks, as you will have them for a very long time. Selling these stocks will increase your annual income, which may push you into a higher tax bracket, or take away your eligibility for other tax deductions. It's for these reasons that I only invest "buy and hold forever" stocks in a general brokerage account.

So what about real estate? You need the right personality to be a landlord. Real estate can be a massive undertaking, but you can potentially reap massive rewards. It's safe to say that **a majority of the richest Americans own a large amount of realty**. It is the ultimate way of leveraging your money. You can buy a piece of real estate with only 20% down, but build equity on the full value of the piece, while having renters pay the mortgage. It is certainly not without its risks, such as was the case during the housing crisis of 2008. Many properties became valued for less than their mortgages, which is called "being underwater" on a loan. If you were forced to sell at the worst time, you actually had to pay money to sell the property. Granted, that doesn't happen every day. In fact, the housing crisis was one of the biggest opportunities of all time to invest in real estate. Many people became millionaires by taking advantage of the housing crisis.

If you want to pursue real estate, there are entire libraries written on the subject. Read all you can, then find someone who has successfully done it, and learn everything you can from them. There are even courses designed to teach you the ins and outs of real estate investing. Do your homework before taking the plunge.

You may be overwhelmed with all of this right now. You may not think you're ready to invest. You may be wanting to just keep plugging money into a savings account because it's the easy way to go. If you do, you are throwing your Ace away! You have a gift that is given to you, the gift of time, which others can only dream of having. You are losing time every year, whether you like it or not. **It may be the hardest years in your life right now to save, but you must do it. Your future depends on it!** Do not throw your Ace away! Save, and then save some more. Save until it hurts! Save until you have to make daily sacrifices. That is when you know you are saving enough. Take what you save, and start investing. **Invest early and invest often.**

CHAPTER 16: STOCKS

So let's dive into the world of stocks. What is a stock again? A stock is a piece of a company. It is not merely a piece of paper or a percentage on a computer screen. It is much more than that. **By owning a share of a company, you are owning a piece of that company.** Be proud of that! Once you understand this and fully grasp it, everything else will start to fall into place.

If you cannot be proud of the stock that you own, you need to question yourself why you own that stock. If you are morally against perpetuating cigarettes or alcohol, then don't invest in companies that produce those products. Begin by investing in companies that interest you or share your same values. This will help keep you interested in them, which will help you keep up to date on their news reports or market trends. The more you are informed about a company, the better decisions you will make. After you gain some experience, you can begin to broaden your horizon by pursuing other companies (diversification).

Be intimately involved in the stock that you own. For instance, when I bought Pepsi stock, I would only choose Pepsi when I drank soda. When I bought Starbucks stock, I would occasionally visit their stores. Does this make a difference? Probably not. My one can of Pepsi doesn't even account for a measurable difference in Pepsi's profits. So why do this? It creates awareness of the company and again, reinforces the belief of being proud of the stock that you own.

Being involved in a stock can also give you additional perspective. You may have gone to a Starbucks to get a coffee, and may not even remember it. Now imagine that own Starbucks stock. Now you begin to see friendly employees, great customer service, and a consistent quality product. You also notice a line of people during the morning rush. Another time, you might see less people at Starbucks over lunchtime. You might get a bit concerned, but then you notice that Starbucks is beginning to offer some sandwiches and other lunchtime food. You smile because you are seeing Starbuck's ability to adapt and create new sources of revenue in existing stores. You see people pay with Apple pay and notice how easy Starbucks makes it to pay. When you own stock in a company, your perspective completely changes and you notice things you never have before.

You are your best analyst with stocks. You have nobody to answer to, no special interests, and no commission on your recommendations. Keep in mind though, you might be wrong. Don't be afraid of being wrong. In fact, use the times of being wrong as a learning experience. For example, I literally could not go anywhere without seeing someone wearing Under Armour. Seemed good to me. I compared Under Armour (David) with Nike (Goliath), and I went with the underdog, hoping it had more potential for growth than the behemoth Nike. It grew and grew for years, and I was feeling good. Then came October of 2016 when Under Armour announced they weren't going to grow as fast as they have been. Sports Authority, one of Under Armour's main distributors, shut down. Under Armour's stock tanked and many sold their shares, causing it to drop further. I still really like Under Armour, and I continue to believe in their products. I'm in it for the long haul. The bottom line is this: as long as you have some basic knowledge of the stock you're investing in, trust your instincts.

Don't buy stock in companies who rely on a single product. Successful companies are able to branch into several markets, creating diversity and a steady revenue stream, regardless of the economic environment. Take 3M for example. They make countless products that have become staples for graphics, electronics, healthcare, home, entertainment, manufacturing, industry, office, safety, government, and all aspects of transportation. They have extensive research & development to help create new products. Contrast this to a company such as

GoPro, who relies on a single product category of action cameras. Although they had a 3rd quarter 2014 revenue of $280 million, I was amazed when their stock fell 12% overnight after Apple was awarded an action camera patent. GoPro has massive name recognition with action cameras, but their stock fell 12% based on the slightest whisper of competition from Apple, who didn't even have a product to compete yet. That to me is a house built on a foundation of sand. This was also a red flag to GoPro, who has since branched into drones and expanded their software interface to make an entire user experience, rather than just a company with a camera. This was a great example of a company realizing a problem, then pivoting to correct it. Of course, this still all depends on the assumption that people's lives are interesting enough to film.

Choose stocks you understand. If a business sounds too complicated, you don't know what they do or how they make money, you won't have a good sense of the value of the company. It will become difficult to follow and you won't know how to trade it. Keep it simple and invest in companies you know and understand. You don't need to know how to create a computer to invest in Apple, but you should be able to explain to a child what that company does, what its goals are, and how it makes money.

Choose businesses with a good pile of cash on hand. Cash is king in the business world and if a business has enough of it on hand, it can weather economic storms, invest in opportunities that arise, or even acquire new companies themselves to produce new revenue streams or enhance their own. Large amounts of cash are a sign of healthy management practices and generally good quality companies. Apple is famous for its cash hoard. Other examples include Cisco, Microsoft, IBM, Oracle, and Google.

Choose companies with high profit margins. This is a sign of a company who typically has a great product both high in demand and superior in quality, a devoted following, brand recognition, with a wide economic moat. Apple is a great example of this.

Choose companies with recession-proof products. Even during the worse of recessions, people will need toothpaste. There's a safe bet that people will still be purchasing alcohol as well. There will always be garbage to haul, and the world will always be at war.

Warren Buffett is famous for saying **"I'd rather buy a good company at a fair price, than a fair company at a good price."** Don't just look for companies at bargain prices. You may be excluding some very good companies by doing this. According to Warren Buffett, timing the market can be very difficult. In fact, he recommends not trying to time the market. Countless research has shown that **you will lose if you try to time the market**. In fact, **the more often you trade, the more likely you will lose money**. If you invest in solid companies and hold them long term, you don't need to time the market. If you have a good entrance strategy, you don't need to worry as much about an exit strategy.

Choose a company with a great leader with a clear vision. You are making a mistake if you do not know anything about a company's CEO. Amazon could not be Amazon without Bezos. Microsoft could not have been Microsoft without Bill Gates. Facebook couldn't have been what it is without Zuckerberg. Tesla wouldn't be Tesla without Elon Musk. To prove this point, just look at what happens when a great leader leaves a company. Apple began to falter when Jobs left, as did Starbucks when Schultz left. Both companies returned to their glory when they returned and have been solid since. Great leaders also choose great successors to carry on their clear vision, as Steve Jobs did with Tim Cook.

Be careful of companies with too much scale. Scale alone is not enough to make a company succeed. **Companies need to maintain the agility to pivot in this rapidly changing market.** As technology advances and new products emerge, so do customer's wants. If a company is too heavily invested in something and cannot adapt, they will quickly become irrelevant. Take, for example, Blockbuster, who did not see the internet coming, and quickly went bankrupt. Of course it is every company's desire to grow, but it's a big red flag if quality or relevance is sacrificed for the sake of growth.

The quality of a company often comes down to its people. **Invest in companies that hire the best, and treat their employees great.** One example is Netflix, who hires the best, gives them independence to make decisions, and pays top dollar. The result is a company with vast scale, agility, and a great product. It is no wonder that Netflix is the "N" in the "FANG" stocks, which together are strong enough to move the global market.

It is dangerous to have more than 5% stake in the business you currently work for. Enron was an energy, commodities, and services company based out of Texas in the 90's. Fortune magazine named Enron "America's Most Innovative Company" and was on the list of the 100 best companies to work for in America. It was touted as a great company with great benefits. Many of its 20,000 employees had their life savings tied up in Enron. Disaster struck for these employees when Enron filed for bankruptcy in 2001 after years of fraud and corruption were exposed. Not only did these employees lose their jobs, but also their entire savings. By limiting your exposure to your business to 5% or less, you are safeguarding against the perfect storm of losing both your job and your savings simultaneously.

Why not mutual funds?   Again, it depends on your investing style. Many 401(k) plans are limited to mutual funds or index funds. In the accounts that I manage specifically, I feel that I get more control with individual stocks than with mutual funds. It's hard for me to identify with a fund called "Mid-cap global fund" rather than a stock called Disney. Stocks make investing personally more exciting for me, so I tend to follow them more closely and become more involved. I also try to minimize fees, which are commonly high with mutual funds. These fees will take a big bite out of your earnings. In fact, **it is hard for any mutual fund to beat the S&P, once you take fees into account.** Mutual fund fees are called expense ratios. Go through your 401(k) and search for funds with expense ratios of 0.25% or less. You'll be surprised to see you're probably paying expense ratios of > 1% in funds that do not outperform funds with expense ratios of < 0.25%! When in doubt, low cost index funds are the way to go in your 401(k), such as Vanguard index funds.

Active mutual funds will always lose to indexing. "It's as certain as night follows day," says John Bogle, founder of Vanguard. What does that mean? Mutual funds that are actively being traded by managers have been proven to lose to passive index investing. Avoid actively traded mutual funds at all costs.

CHAPTER 17: THE VALUE OF A STOCK

The stock market generally increases 7 to 9% annually, faster in bull markets, slower in bear markets. In fact, it's hard to not make money in the U.S. stock market. **Perhaps the best way to ensure great gains is to NOT overpay for a stock.** This means buying stock with a great value. This is easier said than done. There are many ways to tell if a stock is a bargain or not.

So how do you tell if a stock has value? Some stocks, such as Twitter, are difficult to place value on. Value can be obtained one way by looking at a stock's earnings. Just looking at earnings may be difficult to compare stock to stock, but a price to earnings ratio (P/E ratio) helps with that problem.

The P/E ratio is the stock price divided by the earnings per share.

The P/E ratio reflects how much someone is willing to invest to earn $1. For example, if a stock has a P/E ratio of 22, an investor is willing to invest $22 to earn $1. The average market P/E ratio changes frequently, but it is between 20 and 25. A high P/E ratio means people are willing to invest more money, in hopes of higher future earnings. A low P/E ratio means a company either has been doing really well, or is undervalued. Some companies have no P/E ratios, which means either their investors do not earn anything, or the company has lost a lot of money.

You can look at the earnings per share (EPS) individually, but avoid looking at estimated (future) EPS numbers. You care about what the stock is doing right now. After all, **past performance does not guarantee future earnings, but when looking at past performance, focus on recent past rather than distant past.**

The compound growth of a stock is commonly expressed as the **compound annual growth rate**, or **CAGR**. Be careful when looking at this number. Think of it as a smoothed overview of how a stock performed. A stock or a fund may tote their high CAGR, but it does not reflect volatility. **In order to compare the CAGR between stocks, you must use the same time period.** You must also take into account volatility. This gets complicated quickly. In fact, let's not focus on CAGR to determine the quality of a stock.

With any investment you make, you must consider its **return on investment**, or ROI. This is more than a dollar figure. If you invest in a stock that causes you significant stress, such as wild price fluctuations, huge debt, or dropping dividends, its ROI is relatively low in my opinion, and not worth it.

Suppose a business is made which creates a great new app. The business was started by a couple of friends who each own a percentage of the business. Suppose the business now wants to expand and needs some extra cash to do it. They, in turn, will create new shares and sell them. This is called an **initial public offering** (or IPO). Let's say you buy a **share** in this business. You now own that **stock**. Business continues to do well and the stock price increases. The original founders want to make their company more desirable, hoping that people will continue to buy more shares, so they offer a **dividend**. A dividend is a portion of the businesses' profits, distributed to the shareholders. That's you! This is great, because not only do you get a dividend, but you also have the value of the shares (which can fluctuate quite widely, as you will see).

The dividend is often expressed as a percentage. Careful with this number. More on that later. The dividend growth rate, or **DGR**, is compound growth associated with dividends. This is the rate at which a dividend increases. You should also be careful when comparing the DGR between stocks and make sure they reflect the same time period.

You can see, this gets complicated quickly. It is not very easy to calculate or graph out the true value of a company, much less predict what it will do in the future. Professionals who spend countless hours poring over data will still get it wrong. Millions of investors' dollars are lost daily due to wrong predictions of analysts and fund managers. So how do you stand a chance?

It's time to remind you that you are not going to get rich overnight. This is the flip side of the power of time. **It takes a long time to take advantage of the power of time**. It also takes a great deal of discipline. As Jocko Willink says, "Discipline creates freedom." Maintaining financial discipline will give you freedom from financial stress. Help yourself maintain discipline by automating your savings. Learn to live on less. Create automated monthly transfers from your checking to your savings, Roth IRA, or other brokerage accounts. Just don't forget to invest it once it's in that account! Got a pay raise? Great! Since you're living on less, you can dedicate those raises to your investments.

So what kind of investor are you going to be? You will come to learn that there are many methods and styles of investing. One way may not be better, just different. Much like people's personalities. In fact, your personality will reflect which method of investing best suits you. You will find strengths and weaknesses in all types. There are analytical investors, who study charts, graphs and numbers, and can see things that the rest of us can't. There are also behavioral investors who are able to disconnect their emotions from their investments. They see opportunity when others are running for the exit. You may think this seems easy, but wait until you're in that situation. There are investors who invest-and-forget, day traders and long-term holders. There are trading options, hedge funds, index funds, mutual funds, bonds, venture capital, and the list goes on. Before you jump into this world, you must read some books. I suggest books from each type of trading and see what suits you best. Whatever you choose, find some friends you can discuss stocks with. Challenge each other. The more you discuss and throw around ideas, the better off you will be.

Back to determining the value of a stock. **The best way to help minimize risk is to buy undervalued good companies.** Determining what is undervalued, and what is a good company, requires some skill.

You can compare P/E ratios from stock to stock to help compare and determine relative value. By value, I mean determining if the company stock is "on sale" or not. It does NOT tell you the actual value of the company. Investing in stocks with little value is more like speculating. Speculating is investing in a company that you think will gain a disproportional amount of value.

Think you're not a speculator? When you fill your tank with gas because the price is $1.99/gallon and you're afraid it will be more than $2 next week, you are speculating. When you buy extra supplies when they are on sale, you are speculating that the price won't be cheaper than the current sale price. When you buy items on Black Friday, you are speculating that it won't be cheaper on Cyber Monday. We speculate every day. Speculating is fine, as long as you are aware of the increased risks associated with doing so. When starting out, stay away from speculating and choose stocks with value (stocks that are affordable relative to their earnings). Typically choose stocks with a P/E ratio of 20 or less, 15 is best.

Don't rely solely on P/E ratios! We are now going to try to find out a true value of a company. There is a critical flaw in P/E ratios that you must know. P/E ratios do not take into account the level of debt a company has. You need to look that up on your own, or you can use another valuation called the EV-to-EBITDA ratio. EV stands for "Enterprise Value" and is the calculated value a company has. It's a number a banker would look at in the event of a corporate takeover. It is calculated with the following numbers:

EV = Market Cap (which is the total value of outstanding shares) + Total Debt + Preferred Stock (stock with a higher claim on assets and earnings) + Minority Interest (the portion of stock not owned by the parent company) - Cash

But you don't just want to know what a company is worth. You want to take its worth in consideration to what it earns. Basically, you want an inexpensive company that earns big. You will occasionally find a gem when investor's emotions are volatile, which falsely lowers share price. This happens all the time. For example, in May of 2016, Apple's stock dropped to 2 year lows after a report of decreasing iPhone sales. This emotional drop ignored the fact that Apple has a $230 billion cash hoard and is the single most profitable U.S. company. Buy a good quality company when others are afraid. Apple was up 27% less than 5 months later. That price drop was a fire sale to buy more stock.

The EBITDA number is the "Earnings Before Interest, Taxes, Depreciation and Amortization", which is the earnings available to shareholders. **With the EV/EBITDA ratio, the lower the number, the better.** The current median EV/EBITDA ratio for the S&P 500 is about 11.4, so you want a stock with a lower number (cheap company in relation to high earnings and low debt).

Compare stock prices in relation to their P/E ratios and past performance rather than the actual stock price. You cannot compare company A with a stock price of $10 to company B with a stock price of $100 without knowing additional information. **Just because a stock may be more expensive, does not mean it is a better quality stock or has better performance.** You may see much greater gains by having 1 share of a $400 stock than you would with 400 shares of a $1 stock. Knowing that, however, a $1 stock only needs to gain 20 cents for 20% profits, whereas a $400 stock needs to gain $80 for the same return. This is where volatility comes into play. Keep this in mind when looking at past share prices.

Stock value of quality companies will continue to grow with time. I'm sure you'd love to be one of the original shareholders of

Starbucks, Google, Apple, or Facebook. As those businesses grew, the original share value grew exponentially.   Getting in on the ground floor of the next Apple is going to be unlikely, but you don't have to get in on the ground floor. Who knows what Apple will be like 20 years from now? Kids in the year 2035 may look back and only dream of what could have been if they had only invested in Apple in 2017! Remember though, just because a company is a quality company, it can still be overpriced.

Now when someone says "I don't buy stocks more than $300 because they're too expensive," you can just smile because you now know that a high stock price is doesn't necessarily mean it is overvalued. **Price is different than value!** Don't think for a second that a $10 stock is cheaper than a $300 stock. When looking at earnings and stock price history, that $300 stock may be the best value around, and the $10 stock may be way overpriced!

Bottom line is to get to know quality companies, buy on the dips, and hold them forever. **Remember, time is the Ace up your sleeve, so use it to your advantage!**

A quick word on the history of the dollar. **Stock price is all relative to the U.S. dollar, but the U.S. dollar changes its value with time.** This means that a historical stock price may have a different value than it really appears, based on how strong the dollar was at that time. For example, gold is measured in the U.S. dollar. If gold drops in price, but the dollar increases in value based on foreign currencies, the value of gold suddenly appears very different than if you just considered historical price alone. This creates a hidden association you may not have seen before. Sometimes it makes more sense to compare a stock relative to another similar stock, such as oil vs. natural gas or gold vs. silver, to make these hidden associations more visible.

CHAPTER 18: TRADING STOCKS

It has been proven that a majority of investors do WORSE the MORE they trade. **Most investors will perform BETTER the LESS they trade!** How is this possible? Because emotion can get the best of us. When stocks start dropping, it's easy to freak out and follow the herd, selling only to lock in a loss. Once the market rebounds, confidence builds and we begin to buy. We may even buy at a price higher than what we sold! This is the exact OPPOSITE of what we need to train ourselves to do. There are many ways to avoid this trap. Buying quality dividend growth stocks and not looking at your stocks on a daily basis, are two of the best ways to avoid emotional trading. That being said, don't just buy a stock and bury your head in the sand. There are certainly times when a stock should be sold. Back to that later.

This is a reminder. **Be careful to place the correct stocks in the correct investment vehicle.** Stocks that you may consider selling short (< 1 year) belong in a Roth IRA where you do not pay capital gains taxes on the trades (as long as you leave that money in the Roth). Stocks that are buy-and-hold-forever belong in a general brokerage account, where capital gains are taxed when stocks are traded.

Buy and sell stocks strategically. If you have a poor stock you want to dump, but also want to reap some profits off of a great stock, it is a good idea to sell some poor stock at the same time. Taxes allow you to take the capital loss off of the amount of capital gain, thus reducing the amount of taxes paid on your profits. Two birds, one stone.

Consider donating a poor doing stock rather than selling it outright. If you plan on donating money anyway, but also want to dump a poorly performing stock, consider donating the stock itself to charity. This allows you to dodge paying capital gains taxes, you get to take a donation deduction, and a charity still gets a donation with cash value and can do what it wants with it. Everybody wins.

Buy low, sell high. You've heard this before, but what does it mean? The best time to buy stocks are when they are at their lowest, which is generally when they are hated and feared. The best time to sell stocks are when they are at their high, when everyone loves it and wants to be part of it. This may seem like an easy concept to understand, but when you're in the thick of it and see triple digit growth rates, you will want to buy more. **Don't be too greedy.** You can't go wrong by taking a profit, but you can be very wrong by trying to take a very big profit. The trick is to know when to get out.

Before you buy a stock, have an exit strategy in mind. Although we love to buy and hold forever, sometimes that isn't the best course. Do not just buy a stock and rely on hope alone. Hope is not a strategy. Determine a stock price you would sell at and stick to it. If you don't, you'll always come up with an excuse not to sell. It's far too easy to get greedy. Stick to your original exit strategy, because that strategy was made during an unemotional time. Set your alerts to tell you when a stock is high or low. You can set a stop order to minimize losses, and a sell limit order to take your profits.

Don't catch a falling knife (a falling stock). Well, you can, but just be careful. It's best to **wait for the stock to rebound.** When you are looking to buy stocks at their low, wait for them to bounce back up a bit. If you don't do this, they could continue to drop much lower than you anticipate. Be patient and wait for the rebound. Your gain may be less, but you certainly won't lose as much in a downfall. An example is the crash of oil in 2014. Many oil companies were at ridiculously low prices, causing many to jump into these stocks, only to have them continue to fall through 2015. If you don't know where the bottom of the lake is, don't jump in!

A famous quote by Baron Rothschild is "**The best time to buy is when there's blood in the streets**." Along those same lines is a quote by Warren Buffett, "**Be fearful when others are greedy, and be greedy when others are fearful**."

Sir John Templeton, who is called the greatest investor of the 20th century, put all of his money he had saved, and even borrowed some additional money, into stocks in 1939. This was during the Great Depression and the start of WWII, when there literally was blood in the streets. It took guts, and this investment became the basis of his vast fortune. This allowed him to fund research in science and technology, resulting in innovations so large that Queen Elizabeth knighted him.

So how do you know when to sell a stock? **There are a few red flags that should alert you to start to consider selling.** If you are not following the news about your stocks, you may miss these red flags. There are plenty of stock tracking apps and email newsletters available that make following business news fast and easy. My favorites are Seeking Alpha, Daily Trade Alert, and the Yahoo Financial app. I also will research stocks on websites like Yahoo! Finance and CNN Money. Things I consider red flags are:

1) When a stock suddenly stops paying a dividend, or drastically reduces its dividend. Don't immediately sell when you see this, since that company may have a very good reason why it did that. Find out why first. Overall, your goal is to hold stocks with increasing dividends, so a decreasing dividend is a huge red flag.
2) When a dividend is > 9%, I start to worry that this is a dangling carrot to keep investors, which makes me wonder why they need to dangle a carrot in the first place. On the other hand, when a stock price plummets, but the dividend remains the same, the result is an increasing dividend yield percentage without actually increasing the dividend. That is

why it is important to always look at the stock price in relation to its dividend.

3) When a stock becomes overvalued or seems to bubble. When everyone loves the stock and when analysts all are screaming "Buy!" start to worry that it has reached a bubble.
4) When a CEO leaves unexpectedly, if there are mass layoffs, or a spin off occurs.
5) When there has been 200 days or longer with no gains.
6) When there is a drop in 10% of the share value. Caution though, this may be a great time to buy more stock if you believe in it, and its fundamentals are solid.

Never use just one of these red flags to make a decision. Take all the factors into account. Keep in mind that it's not just the red flags that tell you when to sell. **Remember, when you sell a stock, you don't need to sell all of it.** If you are still very happy with the stock, you may want to reap your profits. If you are up 100% in a stock, consider selling half. This is a very common and very successful practice to follow. Why do this?

- You are securing your profits. You now have your entire initial investment back and are free to invest in another stock.
- You have lowered your risk by not having so much tied up in a single stock, and your profits have allowed you to further diversify.
- You still have left half the money in, which was your initial investment, allowing it to continue to ride and realize any further upside potential.
- You have taken emotion out of the equation by making this a standard practice.

What date should I buy or sell on? There are two main dates to be aware of when trading: the Record Date and the Ex-Dividend Date. **The Record Date is the day you need to own that stock in order to receive its dividend.** You want to own that stock at least three days prior to that date. It would be a shame to be considering buying a stock, then to miss out on this date and a dividend payment for a year. **The Ex-Dividend Date is the date that determines if you get the next dividend or not.** This date is typically two days before the record date. You want to buy before this date, and only sell after it.   Even if you sell after this date and no longer own shares, you will still get that dividend. After the Ex-Dividend date, you may notice the stock price falling a bit. This is because of sell-offs that occur after the date. The price typically recovers as new buyers want the next dividend.

A value trap is a stock that is priced low enough where it appears to be a good value. Digging a bit deeper, you may find this perceived value is not a value at all, but a trap. So, **how do you tell a bargain from a value trap?** Here are some tips to follow:

- Entire distressed sectors are likely value traps. (Ex: oil crash, real estate housing crisis)
- A one-time crisis usually is a bargain. (Ex: Wells Fargo account scandal of 2016)
- When a company appears weak for no apparent reason, it's likely a value trap.

You can't go broke taking profits, but you can make a whole lot more if you continue to ride the wave. As we saw before, if you have a winning stock, you may want to sell a portion of the stocks to take some profit, then reinvest those profits into other bargain stocks to help diversify. You can't really lose by doing this, but you can really limit your gains. It's more risky, but if you want to enjoy serious triple digit gains, stick with the stock longer than is comfortable. This is an example where you may want to use a stop-loss to help protect your profits.

Riding the wave of profit is very different than sticking with an overvalued stock. It is important to recognize the difference. If the company is making great profits legitimately, with a valuable product or service, then stick with it. If the company is making great profits because it is the emotional flavor of the day, it is in danger of being overvalued. When a stock is overvalued, it is a good time to reap your profits early and diversify.

CHAPTER 19: MARKET CORRECTIONS

"I'm afraid that sometimes you'll play lonely games too. Games you can't win, 'cause you'll play against you." Dr. Seuss

Markets go up (bull market), and markets go down (bear market). When we think of risk in an investing sense, we think of losing all of our money. Risk is more than this. Risk is not only the potential of losing principle, but also losing dividends and losing growth potential. Risk is market volatility. So how do you protect yourself and mitigate risks? There are several ways.

Use stop losses, maybe. Stops are set-points that trigger a stock sale when it reaches a certain value. Many people use these stops to help protect their initial investment. I don't like a stop unless I know I want to sell a stock, and am just waiting until the price starts to fall a bit.   I use these for more volatile stocks. Once they have reached a certain level where I'm comfortable taking the profit, I'll place a stop loss at about 5 to 10% below that price. If the stock continues to climb, I'll increase my stop loss. This can be done automatically with something called a trailing stop. **It's easy to make money in a bull market. It's hard to NOT to lose money in a bear market, but stop losses can help mitigate your losses.**

With some stocks, I do not place a stop loss. It's important to remember that one usually fails when trying to time the market. I'm a long term investor who invests in good solid companies whom I have faith in. If the stock price is dropping, I may consider it going on sale and may end up buying more! **My safety net is diversification** amongst many sectors: energy, industrial, biotech,

tech, etc. If one sector performs poorly for a time, chances are it is when another sector is doing well.

Don't panic! When markets free fall, it is easy to panic and want to sell off, in attempts to try to preserve any sort of principal. A true investor would view a free fall market as a Black Friday sale, where quality stocks are being sold at incredible values. Just don't catch a falling knife. I learned this the hard way. I invested in Amazon, in hopes to make a quick buck. Amazon stock was very volatile and unpredictable at the time. Within two weeks, I lost 20% of what I invested. I panicked and sold, taking the loss, afraid to lose anymore.   The very next day, the stock turned around. Within a month, it was right back to what I had bought it for, then it continued to climb. I would have been better off not even looking at the stock price and waiting.

Remember, it's proven research that the more you trade, the more you lose. Relax, don't panic. **Don't believe the financial news, they are just as emotional as the market** and tend to focus on and attempt to explain statistically insignificant changes. It's funny when I hear "Apple dropped 1.2% on news of reduced iPhone sales, blah, blah, blah." Ignore the speed bumps and look to the horizon. **Remember, the trend is your friend. Focus on the trend, not the speed bumps. Keep your finger on the overall pulse of the economy and learn to recognize market trends.**

Do not look at stocks daily. Remember, you're in it for the long haul. Don't let the daily news give you the jitters. It's too tempting to buy and sell based on daily changes, so don't even look at them on a daily basis. Monitoring your stocks every month or two is a good rule of thumb. This helps smooth out the bumps in the road and keep your eyes on the horizon.

Don't be afraid of bubbles. Don't rush off and sell if analysts are calling a particular stock a bubble. It may be a bubble, but stocks in bubbles usually continue to increase much longer than anticipated. If you sell too early, you could easily miss out on 20% gains.

Instead, this is the one area you may employ stop losses. I'm usually not a big fan of stop losses, unless you want to sell the stock anyway. Place a stop loss within 10% of the current stock price in that situation. If it continues to go up, adjust your stop loss along the way. If the stock tanks, be thankful that you sold within 10% of its peak.

You can always change your allocations to more conservative holdings. **A good rule of thumb is to hold at least 20% of your allocations in stocks, but not more than about 80%.** The rest should be bonds, real estate investment trusts, etc.

During bull markets, focus more on large cap value stocks. There are two main categories of stocks: growth and value.
- Growth stocks are those with the potential to grow and outperform the overall market.
- Value stocks are those who are undervalued and are trading at a level below what they are really worth.

Value stocks are considered a bit more risky, as something negative has influenced its public perception and thus has driven down the stock. But, as the news cycle changes, public perception may also change, and the value stock suddenly surges, creating a great return. This isn't always the case, however. Remember the value trap?

There are small, mid, and large cap stocks, which can fall into either the growth or value category. Large cap stocks are stocks with a market capitalization of greater than $10 billion. They tend to weather storms better than small cap stocks, but may experience slower growth than small or mid-cap stocks.

Large cap value stocks are great, if you can find them. This is what Warren Buffett refers to as "hunting for a whale".

Patience, patience, patience! The more patient you are with stocks, the better your investments will be. If you are able to take the emotional pull out of trading decisions, you will be much better off for it. About every five to seven years there is a significant market correction, typically about a 20% drop in stocks. About every ten years, there is a major market correction, or a crash, which may be isolated to a particular sector (tech crash in October of 2002, for example). A patient investor will ride out these storms. An unemotional investor will buy more! If they are good quality companies, think of crashes like a fire sale, an opportunity that may pay off big time.

If you flipped a coin nine times and got heads each time, what is the chance you'll get heads on the 10th flip? It is still a 50/50 chance. **Stocks do not have a predetermined life span in bull markets.** As some stocks continue to climb to all-time highs, some investors will get nervous if several months go by without a correction. This leads them to think that a major correction is in store, and they bail out. Back to flipping a coin, it's still a 50/50 chance, even after the first nine flips. If you bail out of a bull market too soon, you're missing out on big time gains.

Rahm Emanuel once said "**Don't let a crisis go to waste.**" Sounds cold hearted, but there is a good lesson here. Take, for example, the 2010 oil spill in the Gulf of Mexico. Many offshore drilling stocks plummeted > 30%. Your knee jerk reaction would be to sell and save whatever capital you can, even if it was at a loss. If you had stop losses in place, you would have sold and preserved your initial capital. But if you held, you would find any losses to have recovered in a matter of months. If you took Warren Buffett's advice and bought more when everyone was running away, you would see an additional 25% in profits.

Accidents happen and emotions can sway stock prices very quickly, but it doesn't mean you need to get caught up in the emotions too. Good quality stocks will maintain their value and come back, sometimes even stronger. Remember the previously noted quote "Buy when there is blood in the streets." **Bear markets are great opportunities to buy quality stocks at bargain prices.**

This is exactly why **you should never just cash out and leave the market.** Even if you do, and miss a major correction, who is going to tell you where the bottom is and when to get back in? Oftentimes, the upswing is missed, and you're stuck paying taxes on what you sold.   If you cash out and the market keeps going up, you've just missed that too. **Market timing rarely works.** It frequently results in stress and loss of capital. Just settle down and don't let your emotions get the best of you.

CHAPTER 20: STOCK ALLOCATION

Diversify based on age, maybe. When you're older, having a good mixture of bonds, real estate, and dividend paying stocks can help ensure cash flow during retirement, which can reduce the need to sell off stock if stock prices happen to be low at that time. Quality stocks will still pay the same dividend, even during recessions when the market is low.

Some people will allocate 100% of their portfolio into stocks. If you're young, you may think to invest more in growth stocks to try to take advantage of potential rapid growth, then diversify more into large cap value stocks, bonds, and real estate when you're older. Doing this can get things kick started early on. You may be able to afford to take higher risks, since retirement is far off and you will not be forced to sell if a market correction occurs. There is a huge disadvantage by doing this though.

Loading up on pure stocks (100% stock allocation) goes against the grain of many of the most successful investors of all time, and for good reason. **You can't take advantage of compound growth if you lose it all.** Ray Dalio, and several other famous investors, get much of their success by **focusing on not losing**. This means diversification, more than pure stocks. In fact, they recommend only about 30% of your portfolio to be in stocks. The rest should be in gold, US Treasury bonds, US Treasury inflation-protected securities (TIPS), foreign developed equities, foreign emerging-market equities, and real estate investment trusts (REITs). Another quote by Warren Buffett, "**There are 2 rules to investing. Rule number 1 is to not lose money. Rule number 2 is to follow rule number 1.**" As you get older and approach retirement, you do not want to be forced to sell stocks when the market is down. That is why it is very important to develop a strategy for some degree of constant cash flow from your diversified investments, right from the beginning, and take advantage of compound growth by reinvesting that cash flow.

What stocks do you choose? Many say that you cannot beat an index fund that tracks the S&P 500, which is about 7% annually. In fact, Warren Buffett placed a million dollar bet that a group of hedge fund managers could not beat that index fund, and they failed. Investing in individual stocks is much more risky than an index fund, but the rewards have the **potential** of being much greater. Key word is potential. Whether that actually pans out or not is up to you. I certainly have had gains of 150 - 200% a year in some stocks, but have also lost 10 - 20% in some years. Does this average to more than 7% annually over all the years? So far, yes. But history tends to repeat itself, and recessions are bound to happen again.

Invest in some world dominating stocks. By this I mean businesses who have a global reach and completely dominate one sector. These stocks will still provide great returns for relatively low risk, as they are usually well diversified themselves. When you look at the big picture, it is not the biotech stocks that will make you the most money. It is these good old-fashioned reliable quality world dominating stocks. These stocks will be able to withstand economic downturns because of their reach and diversification, and therefore will be able to still pay a dividend. Some will even continue to increase their dividend in the face of recessions! Examples include Coca-Cola, Colgate-Palmolive, Exxon, and Procter & Gamble. These stocks have been paying solid reliable dividends for over 100 years and will likely continue to do so.

Boring is big money. Keep about 75% to 90% of your stocks in good, solid, boring companies. Boring companies are those who won't go out of business when new technologies emerge. These are Procter & Gamble, Johnson & Johnson, Walmart, Pepsi, Coke, etc. These are good, reliable, safe stocks who pay increasing dividends over the years. These are "buy and forget" type stocks. **Remember, all you have to be is an average investor to make great long term gains with boring companies.** You can use the remaining 10% to 25% of your stocks on what I call "wild cards". These are stocks who may or may not pay a dividend, but are utilizing current technology to make loads of cash. Biotechs, such as AbbVie and Regeneron Pharmaceuticals, are examples of companies who have enjoyed big time profits.

It may take a very long time to see good returns from these companies. For example, if a company pays a dividend yield of 3%, you won't see a huge return over just 1 year. But if that same company has a history of raising dividends annually, and continues to do so, in 20 years you could see your yield-on-cost easily become 30% or more. This doesn't even take into account that the company will likely continue to grow, resulting in an increased value and stock price. That is solid, reliable, relatively low risk gains, but **you have to start now** to get that ball rolling.

Invest in companies with a wide economic moat. These are companies with strong brand recognition in common household goods. There may be plenty of generic brand competitors, but people continue to reach for these dominant brands. For example, would you reach for M&M's, or a generic equivalent? The company Mars benefits from its brand recognition of M&M's, Snickers, Milky Way, etc. Well-known brands typically sell for higher than their generic, giving that company a higher operating margin. If you're buying a box of cereal, chances are that it's from General Mills. You've probably heard of Cheerios, Wheaties, Lucky Charms, Golden Grahams, Progresso, Bisquick, Betty Crocker, Yoplait, and the list goes on. These are all strongly recognized brands, all owned by General Mills. These are examples of strong companies with wide moats. They're safe, reliable, and you would do well to own some of them.

Is it patriotic to invest in the United States? Not only is it supporting your own country, but the United States economy is a dominant engine on which many other countries depend. It feels good to put your money towards businesses who contribute to the American economy and who employ other Americans. Be proud of being part of the greatest country in the world! That being said, diversifying in quality foreign stocks can help ride out the bumps along the way. Again, one way to do this is by investing in American companies with extreme global reach. Take Nike, for example, who has a huge market in Europe. It's an American stock, with global diversification, which trickles down to you. On the other hand, it's also important to have stocks that are just starting to emerge in foreign markets. Under Armour, for example, has only about 5% of foreign exposure at the time of this writing. There is much more growth potential there than Nike, but it will take many years to attain that higher foreign market share.

How long should you hold a stock for? As Warren Buffett says, **"The ideal length of time to hold a stock is forever."** We don't want to be day traders and attempt to anticipate the market. That is a good way to lose a lot of money really quickly. When you buy great stocks, hold onto them and ride out the rocky times. **Your goal should be to continue to accumulate quality stocks that pay a dividend and reinvest those dividends.** By doing this, you don't need to research or follow stocks on a daily basis. Again, it is healthier to not look at them daily. It is easy to get caught in the emotion of daily swings and you may feel the urge to sell. Of course there may be some bum stocks that you'll need to dump, but you can't judge those by daily swings, only long term trends.

Selectively reinvest dividends. When you set up a brokerage account, you designate if you want it a reinvesting account, or a non-reinvesting account. A reinvesting account automatically takes any dividend payments and plugs them back into that same stock, creating compound growth. This is autopilot, which has its advantages. The cash doesn't sit and immediately is put back to work. Stock is repurchased at a variety of highs and lows, which evens out with time.

Alternatively, you can selectively reinvest dividends. In a non-reinvesting account, the cash accumulates. When it reaches a certain level, you have two main options:

1) Go shopping for new stocks. Keep a wish list of stocks you have been following. When a stock you've been watching reaches a good value, buy it.
2) Wait for a dip in the price of the stock that gave you that dividend, then buy more of that stock. This allows for a "buy low" strategy.

Selectively reinvesting dividends is more work, but theoretically is more beneficial than automatically reinvesting. We all know that theory is different than reality though. Life gets busy, you forget to do it, the cash sits there unused, you lose the benefit of compound growth, and the stock price just keeps getting higher. May as well be throwing money away. Make it simple and automatically reinvest the dividends.

A good list to check out is the CCC list, created by David Fish. CCC stands for "Champions, Contenders, and Challengers." Companies who have paid higher dividends for at least 25 consecutive years are Champions, those for at least 10-24 years are Contenders, and those for 5-9 years are Challengers. The list is based on stock price, P/E ratios, and dividends. Don't make the mistake of thinking a company is a good quality company just because it pays a dividend. A quality company is based on many factors, but a lot of the research is already done by looking at this great list of quality companies.

Own a manageable number of stocks in your portfolio. Owning more than 25 stocks is to complicated and time consuming to keep track of. If you are just starting out, start with about five stocks. Add stocks every year until you reach between 20-25 stocks. Once you have reached that point, continue to track these stocks, dump the bad ones, and research new ones. It is always a good idea to have a stock "wish list" and begin to follow those you are wanting to buy. That way when the funds are available, you can be confident when, and if, to pull the trigger.

Diversify your stocks across various sectors. These sectors include banks, tech, energy, consumables, industry, etc. This diversification will help smooth out any economic bumps along the way. You may feel the urge to focus on one particular hot sector, but diversification is too important to ignore. Just ask anyone who lost everything during the .com bubble. When choosing multiple stocks in one particular sector, choose dueling giants. For example, buying stocks of both Apple and Microsoft, although stiff competitors, will both benefit from each other.

Your stocks will grow at various rates and may become out of balance. It is a general good rule of thumb to avoid >15% of your total portfolio to be represented by a single stock. The exception to this is when you first start out investing. The first stock I ever bought was Apple, which then represented 100% of my portfolio. I continued to diversify over the years and that percentage quickly came down. It's a good idea to check out the percentages of stock holdings in your portfolio annually. Rebalancing means to sell off a portion of the profits of some top performers, followed by buying stocks of lower performers. This may seem backwards, but go back to the rules of "buy low and sell high" and "buy quality companies". **Rebalancing keeps you on track, but don't just do this automatically.** For example, selling a portion of a top performer just before the "Santa rally" during Christmas might mean you missed out on 5% gain. You also would not want to sell just before an ex-dividend date, which is the date when dividends are distributed. If you have your rebalancing on autopilot, these important dates are not factored in, and you may lose out on that income.

CHAPTER 21: DIVIDENDS

Remember, a dividend is the amount paid from a company to its shareholders. It is a way to entice people to buy their stock, which gives more working capital to that company. It's a win-win situation.

Dividends will benefit you. Dividends are predictable income that usually do not change with market volatility. You don't have to do anything to continue to earn a dividend. When you are retired and have multiple dividend paying stocks in your portfolio, you may be able to live off of this dividend income alone. By being able to do this, you aren't forced to sell stock when you don't want to. Although some companies may decrease their dividends, that's a big red flag. Companies will do their best to steadily increase dividends over the years. Again, diversifying in quality stocks will help protect against volatile dividends and ensure a steady income stream.

Dividends are a sign of a healthy company. It takes a lot for a company to pay a dividend, and to be able to maintain that dividend during recessions. It's a sign of a healthy management who values its investors. **Companies that have a history of increasing dividends annually, despite recessions, are a sure sign of a very strong company.** These are the companies that have been shown to outperform the market. An example of this is Coca-Cola. **Companies that raise their dividends annually will outperform companies who do not.** Look for companies who pay a dividend of at least 2.5%, but don't just chase yields.

The one-year percentage return on your investment from the dividend is called the Yield. Don't worry too much about the Trailing Yield, since it's based on historical yields. You care about what the yield is at this moment. So when you look up a stock, find its yield. Yield is the annual dividend divided by the current stock price, thus it fluctuates as the stock price fluctuates. If you already own the stock, you can use your original cost basis (the amount you purchased the stock for) in place of the current stock price to get your individual **Yield on Cost**. This is more of a "feel good number" and is used only to show you how you are doing with that stock over the long haul. It can give you a bit of perspective as to how that stock is performing in relation the price you paid for it.

Dividend yield is expressed as a percentage, not an actual dollar amount. Dividend yield is calculated by dividing the annual dividends per share by the price per share.

Remember, since the price per share constantly varies, the dividend yield also varies. If the company's share price drops, yet it pays the same dividend, the dividend yield percentage suddenly increases. This is why you cannot judge a company based on its dividend yield alone. **Don't fall into the trap of chasing high yields. Always look at yields in relation to the historical stock price.**

What is a dividend payout ratio? When looking at dividend yield, it pays to take into account how much the stock is actually earning. The payout ratio shows the relationship between the dividend and the earnings.

The dividend payout ratio equals the annual dividends per share divided by earnings per share.

This ratio can help determine if the stock has a healthy balance of paying shareholders and reinvesting profits for development or expansion. You may have to dig deep to find this number. If the ratio is too high, the stock may be paying out too much to its shareholders and not reinvesting enough, calling into question the company's ability to maintain that level of dividend. Ratios of >100% are unsustainable. Stable ratios over several years are a sign of a stable company. As with any one number, be careful to not rely too heavily on this number. Earnings can be manipulated, as they can be recorded as early or late, expenses can be pushed back, lines of credit made, etc. Check out the company's cash flow as a way to cross check this.

It is still worth having stocks that don't pay dividends? Some very good companies do not pay dividends. There may be many reasons for this. Dividends are a huge expense for that company. They may instead be investing additional profits for expansion, infrastructure, or research & development to ensure higher gains, market value, or for long term strategic planning. You can't know everything a company is up to, but some of this information should be freely available in news announcements, shareholder meeting reports, or analyst columns.

Some research has shown that **dividend paying stocks still outperform non-dividend paying stocks in the long run.** Although Warren Buffett places a huge value on dividend growing stocks, his own Berkshire Hathaway does not pay one. Why not? He states that his investors are much better off by allowing him to reinvest their earnings, in the form of acquisitions of quality companies, rather than paying out a dividend. He states that their record is satisfactory by doing this. I agree in a sense, and personally believe that up to 25% of your stocks should be in companies who do not pay dividends, but instead are focused on insane growth. Take Amazon for example. They do not pay a dividend and have no reportable earnings to speak of. They spend ridiculous amounts of money on a vast array of projects. Their focus is on dominating market share. They are throwing projects up against a wall, seeing which ones stick, and then develop those. Some say it's way over valued and you should avoid this stock. On paper, buying this stock does not make any sense. On the other hand, Amazon has tremendous long-term potential, which may vastly outweigh their current lack of earnings.

CHAPTER 22: BONDS

Bonds are important to not ignore. Imagine a bond being like a loan where you are the creditor to the government, a corporation, or some other municipality. Bonds guarantee a fixed rate, much like a dividend paying stock. They mature at a specific date, however, which is very different than a dividend paying stock. In general, if interest rates go up, bond prices go down, and vice versa. My advice is to stick with short term bonds and stagger their maturity dates. It may be much better than stashing money in a savings account, where you are virtually paying the inflation rate for the convenience of keeping it there. By staggering maturity dates, you ensure some degree of cash flow if you need accessibility.

So let's learn more about bonds. Corporate bonds are issued by companies, and municipal bonds are issued by state and local governments. Interest rates are typically higher for corporate bonds, but you do not pay federal income tax on municipal bond interest rates. In some cases, you're better off taking a lower municipal bond interest rate to avoid the tax. All municipal bonds should go into a non-retirement account since you don't need to worry about the taxes.

Treasuries are bonds issued by the U.S. government. Treasury bills have a three to six month maturity and treasury notes have a one to ten year maturity. Treasury bonds have maturities up to 40 years. Treasury bills do not earn interest, but instead are bought at a discount. For example, you can buy a $10,000 treasury bill for $9,700 and receive the $10,000 when it matures.

U.S. government bonds are considered very safe, followed by municipal bonds and some quality corporate bonds. Moody's and S&P have a bond rating system to determine the quality of the bond.

So is a low risk bond really low risk? Not really. Let's say you bought a 20 year bond with an interest rate of 4%. Not too bad. But suppose interest rates go up to 6% within a few years. Your money is now stuck in a bond earning only 4%, so your bond has lost value, and you've lost the earning potential of a 6% bond. **As interest rates go up, bond values go down, and vice versa.** Who would want to buy your 4% bond? You could sell it at a discount, but then you lose some of your principal. You could also hold onto it until maturity and be thankful for your 4%. Who knows, there may be a major stock correction and you'd be happy with 4%. Interest rates could even go down, in which case your bond would increase in value. The bottom line is that you just don't know. You're best off keeping your bonds until maturity.

So what is the best bond strategy? Buy bonds generally with 1 year maturities, stagger your bond buying, and pay close attention to interest rates to determine when the best time to buy is. Buy a variety of bonds and only get quality corporate bonds. Don't let high interest rates of junky companies lure you to buy their bonds. They are called junk bonds for a reason.

How can I use bonds for emergency cash? First step is to make a first line emergency fund that is adequate for a car repair, leaky roof, or medical bills. This first line fund is cash in a savings or money market account. The first line emergency fund should be enough to bridge the gap to the second line emergency fund, which is made up of staggered bonds. As the bonds reach their maturities, use those. This is also a good utilization for CD's (certificates of deposits). Your third line of emergency funding could be to utilize some contributions to your Roth IRA. Lastly, you could sell stocks from a general brokerage account. If you are in a crisis and anticipate a long period of time with no cash flow, during your first and second phases of emergency funding, start to pay attention to stock prices and incrementally sell off portions of stocks that are the highest. Alternatively, you can sell any poor performers. If there is a capital loss, no taxes need to be paid.

CHAPTER 23: DANGER!

Options trading and trading on margin can be very risky. You may not only lose your starting principal, but you may end up owing more money! My advice is to avoid this. It's complicated and requires incredible devotion to following stocks. You may hear news stories of those who make millions off of single trades. That doesn't happen frequently, which is why it's news. Although you can win big, the vast majority of options traders do not. I know people who have ended up owing tens of thousands of dollars by doing this. It is very difficult to financially rebound from a loss that big. Options trading is for people who do not have the ace that you do, which is time. There are plenty of safer ways to invest and still make big money, with far less stress. **Stay away from options.**

Don't trust politicians. When a stock depends on laws passed by politicians, or promises made by them, stay away from that stock. Don't trust them, they have too many interests to satisfy. I learned this lesson with TransCanada. Bureaucrats blocked the Keystone Pipeline for years and years, and the stock never did much. Although they still paid a dividend during this time, the lack of increase in share price made it a waste of valuable time. Lesson learned. On the other hand, when Trump was elected in 2016, his promise of infrastructure expansion caused building stocks, such as concrete and steel, to soar. These stocks surged on a promise. That's when I sold my industrial stocks. The market is a very emotional beast that lures you into being emotional as well. Don't fall into this trap. If you happen to own a stock that suddenly finds itself in a political spotlight, sell on the good news and take your profit.

Share buybacks aren't always a good sign. Many investors think that when a company buys a portion of its shares back, it is a good thing. In many respects, it is. Basic law of supply and demand says that when there is less of something that people want, the demand, and thus the value, goes up. This is why share buybacks will frequently trigger an increase in stock price. That's good, right? But if times are so good, why didn't they just increase the dividends? Good question.

Some investors prefer share buybacks rather than dividend increases because they would have to pay taxes on those dividends. On the other hand, taxes are still due when the stock is sold. Remember, company executives are acting, in a sense, just like you, the investor. So why would they buy more of their own stock back when the price is high? One reason could be that they think the current price is a bargain and they have some future product up their sleeve. You have no way of knowing this. What you do know is if they were sitting on a cash hoard when stock prices were much lower. Why didn't they buy some shares back at that time? Do they just want to artificially inflate their stock in hopes of triggering other emotional investors to buy more? Bottom line is that although share buybacks typically increase stock price, that company is buying back its own shares at the wrong time, and that is why you do not want to buy more either. That being said, if the company has more cash than they know what to do with, such as Apple, share buybacks are a good thing due to its tax advantages to a buy-and-hold investor.

Don't listen to analysts. Analysts can frequently be wrong, and they have no incentive to stick their necks out by countering the popular opinion. If they downgrade a stock based on an earnings report before the stock opens, and that stock drops, their downgrade is considered based on the higher stock price, not what it is at the open. Analysts are people too. They may be strongly influenced by other pressures from banks or their own firm's positions. You're best to form your own opinions on stocks. In fact, listen to analysts, but then do the opposite.

Use caution when buying stocks in January, due to the January effect. January is a traditionally strong month for the market since a lot of pension and IRA money gets invested during this time for the New Year. January is also hanging onto the Santa Claus rally from December. Stocks are typically expensive this time of year, so you may want to hold on a bit longer before initiating a new position on a stock. The best historical months to buy stocks are January (oddly enough, but just don't do it), March, April, July, November, and December. If you can't find a good stock to buy at a good value, save that money in an account that is earmarked for stock buying. When the opportunity arises, you want to be ready to pounce. In other words, **you want your treasure chest full when you go to war**! Just don't hold onto the cash for too long. Remember the golden rule, invest early and invest often.

Perhaps the largest factor determining stock price is emotion. **I would argue that 80% of a stock price is based on emotion.** Fear can cause panic and send stocks tumbling for no reason. On the other hand, false optimism and greed can artificially prop up weak stocks. Sometimes it can be very difficult to know which is which, other than having a feeling. I have earned more money based on feelings than I have by trying to analyze stocks through numbers. **Keep your emotions in check, but be acutely in tune to the emotions of other investors and the market.**

Imagine you give a toddler one bite of chocolate cake. He loves it and wants more. You give him another bite. All is good in the world. Now, you give two bites of chocolate cake, but before he can eat them, you take one of them away. He's still getting one bite at a time, but he explodes in a fit as if it's the end of the world.

The market is like a toddler. In late 2016, Under Armour announced a lower than expected growth rate and revenue. The company was still growing, but not nearly as fast as they had before. Some cracks in management emerged and the market responded harshly. The stock price dropped by 50% almost overnight. So what did I do? I was a firm believer in Under Armour, but I had lost a lot of money. I could have followed the market and sold, at least protecting some degree of capital, but I didn't. I could have bought more shares at a perceived bargain, but didn't due to a possible value trap. I still believed in the fundamentals of the company and kept hold of the stock. I did so because I did not over-leverage myself and was well diversified, thus dampening the blow of a 50% stock price drop. I also have the gift of time in that I do not need to sell that stock anytime soon. If it sits for 20 more years, that's fine with me. Time will tell, I suppose. The lesson here is that there is value in keeping your emotions in check and insulating yourself from market tantrums. Oftentimes, buying and holding is the best strategy.

CHAPTER 24: PERSPECTIVE

Keep things in perspective. You already have a lifestyle with more money and opportunity than even the pharaoh of Egypt could ever have imagined. Don't strive to be the richest person in the cemetery. You can find enjoyment with remarkably very little money. When half of the world lives on less than $2.50 per day, I think you can find some enjoyment for less than $5. Enjoy what you have and share it with those less fortunate. **Sharing what you have will actually bring you more enjoyment than spending it on yourself.** Don't believe me? Go to Starbucks and buy some random person a coffee, or bring someone you work with a coffee, and then see how you feel.

CHAPTER 25: WHO TO TRUST

Need more advice? Who do you trust? **Seek out an investment advisor**. An investment advisor is obligated to place your interests first. A financial planner is not. Although there may be many honest financial planners out there, many are beholden to whom they work for, their commissions, or other incentives to push favored stocks. The same with brokers. In short, financial planners and brokers are salesmen. You wouldn't go to a Toyota dealership and expect them to sell you a Honda.

Never, ever, ever give custody of your money to any advisor. Have you heard of Bernie Madoff? His Ponzi scheme robbed hundreds of millions of dollars and left countless people and foundations bankrupt. It is named the greatest financial fraud in history.

One more thing, some independent investment advisors can dually register as a broker as well. That means they can switch between having a fiduciary duty to act in your best interests to a broker looking to sell you something. If you are using an investment advisor, make sure they are not dually registered.

I installed carpet once, and it looked terrible. From then on, I made a decision that it pays to have it professionally installed. So wouldn't we do the same with our finances? Why not just hand over your finances to a professional? The bottom line is that **no one will care more about your finances than yourself**. We can all think of multiple celebrities who have lost massive amounts of wealth by entrusting their finances to a "professional". By taking responsibility of your own finances, you are better able to see what comes in, what goes out, and what changes you can make to improve your own situation. You are better able to see direct results from disciplined living and will thereby become encouraged to do it more. **Take control of your finances, trust yourself, and maintain discipline.**

In summary, live frugally, invest early, invest often, and read a lot.

"You're off to Great Places! Today is your day! Your mountain is waiting, So...get on your way!" Dr. Seuss

34703274R00057

Made in the USA
Middletown, DE
28 January 2019